Writer's First Aid

Getting Organized, Getting Inspired, and Sticking to It

By Kristi Holl

Editor: Mary Spelman

Copy Editor: Cheryl de la Guéronnière

Production: Joanna Horvath

Cover Illustration: Jennifer Hayden

Text Design: Brett Warren

International Standard Book Number 1-889715-31-X
10 9 8 7 6 5 4

1-800-443-6078 www.WritersInstitutePublications.com
Email: Services@WritersBookstore.com
Printed in Canada.

Contents

Introduction

Kristi Holl has been a published writer for over 20 years. Through a dozen surgeries, raising children, a divorce, numerous moves, and several financial crises, she continued to write. As a writing teacher for 17 years, Ms. Holl used her experiences to encourage and advise hundreds of students, many of whom faced a similar challenge—how to integrate their writing with other aspects of their lives. A series of articles on these issues expanded into weekly writing for two websites. Repeated requests from both writing students and published authors for previously published articles convinced her to assemble 40 of her most popular articles into *Writer's First Aid*. While Ms. Holl's experience has been that of a housewife and mother writing primarily for children, her suggestions and solutions apply to *all* writers.

Writer's First Aid is divided into four sections for easy reference: "Getting Started," "Work Habits That Work for You," "Money and Other Practical Matters," and "Creating the Writing Life You Love." When a writer is experiencing a particular problem, he or she can turn to the section of the book covering that topic and find 10 articles. These range from the very practical (in the work habits sections) to inspirational and challenging (in the section on creating the writing life you love). Articles in *Writer's First Aid* fit the busy writer's sched-

schedule: long enough to be helpful, yet short enough to be read during five-minute breaks.

Think of *Writer's First Aid* as a medicine chest, full of good things for what ails many writers. Medicine chests contain items that kill pain, bind up wounds, bring restoration, and increase vitality. May this volume be each of those things to you.

Getting Started

Checkup from the Neck Up

Whatʼs the #1 challenge for new and experienced writers alike? Getting started. The most brilliant writer wonʼt produce a paragraph unless he or she can begin.

My old ʼ87 Ford station wagon was rusted out, had a broken windshield, no turn signals, no tail pipe, and a broken radio. But I drove it for nearly 200,000 miles. Why? Regardless of frigid winter wind chills or blistering summer heat, it always started. Without fail.

If you canʼt start your engine, it doesnʼt matter if you own a junker or a new Porsche. If you canʼt get started writing, it doesnʼt matter if your goal is to pen a two-line jingle or the Great American Novel. The prerequisite is getting started. Essential—for writers and for cars—is a reliable ignition system.

Clunkers and Cadillacs

You, the writer, can develop a surefire ignition system, even if the rest of your "vehicle" has extensive wear and tear. Chances are, your vehicle is not much better or much worse than anyone else's. Few of us drive a stretch limo. So even if you're mad at your boss, have an ulcer, and just argued with your teenager *again*, you must consider these complaints as existing **elsewhere** in the vehicle. Like a car, even with a buckled door, no windshield wipers, and an exhaust pipe dragging on the ground, you can still function if you have a decent ignition system. At the very least, the car will start and you can lurch to the repair shop.

Diagnose the Problem

Do you have trouble starting? First, you need to diagnose your ignition problems. Do a checkup from the neck up. What kind of system do you use to start your writing engine?

(1) Does your engine burst with energy at the turn of the key, but then die the moment you shift the car into gear? Does your car never leave the driveway? Likewise, do you rush to your desk and boot up the computer in a burst of creative energy, then take a break for coffee (or the morning paper, or to walk the dog or call your neighbor) just as the ideas start to flow? Do you never get beyond the opening paragraph?

(2) Or do you pump the accelerator furiously before turning the key and flood the engine with enough gas to drive cross-country? Your engine dies as you choke on gasoline fumes. In a similar way, is your mind flooded with a dozen fantastic ideas, your massive research notes spread over your work surface and dribbling onto the floor? Are you "pumped" when you sit down to write, only to find that your abundance of material overwhelms rather than inspires you?

(3) Or do you grind the ignition, gritting your teeth and pounding the dash as you twist the key

over and over? No matter how long and hard you grind, the engine never starts. Is this also your writing style? When it's time to write, do you grit your teeth and beat yourself up instead? Do you shame yourself into starting by saying things like "You lazy good-for-nothing, get busy!" or "You call yourself a writer?" Does your self-esteem fizzle along with your desire to write?

These ignition systems are worse than worthless, guaranteeing false starts or no starts at all. To stay with a faulty ignition system like any of these—either as a writer or a driver—is pointless and destructive.

A Better Way

If you're going to fulfill your writing dream, you *have* to start. You need to develop a deluxe ignition system and transform yourself from a Writer Wreck to a Rolls Royce Writer. So close your eyes. Relax and breathe deeply. Can you sense in your body what a healthy ignition system would feel like—how it would feel to start a creative project without the drama and angst and hair-pulling?

Can you imagine "easy" writing? Do you recall what it feels like to turn a key in the ignition of a new car with a finely tuned engine? The *effortlessness*. The *quiet*. No need to think about anything. Nothing to fear. You just turn the key . . .

Try to locate that feeling of ease. Feel it. Feel the purring of a quiet, well-maintained engine. You are that engine. Now imagine yourself moving quietly and easily to your computer or work station, sliding smoothly onto your chair, placing your fingers lightly on the keyboard, breathing evenly. With a small smile, you type your first words. You don't open a vein. You don't bleed on the keys, you don't pull your hair. Instead, your engine hums as you fill the screen or paper with words that are perfectly fine for now.

Can you picture such an easy start? Visualize it over and over—whatever your version of a smooth start is—until it's part of your own well-tuned engine. Then, before your feet even hit the floor in the morning, visualize it all over again. Then act it out as you've rehearsed it in your mind.

You've started!

Starting Again

WHEW! Once you start, the problem is over, right? Hardly.

That's because every day you will need to restart many, many times. If you take a break, you have to restart. If your mind drifts to what to cook for supper, you have to restart. If you answer the phone—or even just listen to the answering machine screen your call—you have to start again. Even *without* interruptions, you will have to restart. After taking notes from one source of information, you have to start again when you open the next book or website. At the end of a paragraph, after you decide what to write next, you have to restart.

You will start and restart a million times during the course of writing your first book or making your first magazine sale. So you must learn to start well, and start with *energy*. Don't start out lethargic and defeated, planning only to write a few lines or quit in 20 minutes to watch your favorite talk show. Beginning to write with your first long break already planned is *not* starting with energy.

When you put the key in the ignition, be determined not just to start, but to start with energy. And be committed to continue with energy. *Good* writing requires a full tank of gas. So how's your car running? **Time for a tune-up?**

Hitting a Home Run

I just returned, hot and sweaty, from my fourth-grade daughter's softball game. As I watched the girls hit the ball (some with Twiggy bird-like legs, others more hefty), I realized that I wrote *the same way* they stood in the batter's box. And when I didn't "score" with my writing, it was for the same reasons most of these little girls couldn't get to first base.

Batter Up!

Some of the small batters approached home plate with shuffling, hesitant steps (much as I approach my computer on days when I have a headache). Other players rolled their shoulders, swung the bat, and strutted to the plate (much as I approach my computer on days when "The Muse is IN"). But how the players approached the batter's box made little or no difference as to whether they got on base. The only thing that mattered was what happened when the bat met the ball.

Some girls swung hard and connected with power, but the ball flew sideways over the fence into the stands. FOUL. Others swung timidly and connected with a tiny *pop* that tapped the ball right back to the pitcher, who caught a pop fly or tossed the ball easily to first base. OUT. The only players to get on base did both: give the ball momentum (like the girls who hit hard) and direction (like the girls who hit the ball straight ahead).

It's exactly the same with writers.

Starting Styles

What kind of starting style do you have when you begin your writing day? Are you like the batter who swings hard at every pitch? Do you approach the keyboard with similar energy, ready to dig in and create? Are you convinced that this is the day you'll write that poignant scene with your heroine's grandfather? Do you boil over with enthusiasm for your work?

Then do you get busy and . . . re-label your disks, browse through a writer's magazine, study two catalogues, run to the post office, answer your e-mail, check in with your online writers' chat group, get out your notes about the grandfather, polish your foggy glasses . . . and break for lunch? FOUL.

Or are you like the soft-hitting batter? Do you sidle up to your desk thoughtfully, slowly, methodically? Do you set your mystery novel on the left side of the computer, with your revision notes on the right side? Do you boot up, find the right folder, open the mystery file, and position your blinking cursor? Then do you get busy and . . . plan which bills to pay first, decide what to wear on your evening out, wonder how to prevent your son from getting his body pierced, worry about what to do if the rain doesn't let up and the basement floods again . . . and break for lunch? OUT.

Ya Gotta Have Both

Even though Writer #1 appears to be busy with the myriad tasks of writing, he isn't really writing. Even though he moves quickly and with energy from task to task, he still hasn't written the poignant grandfather scene when his writing time is over. Writer #1 and Batter #1 have the same problem: momentum, but no direction.

And even though Writer #2 is organized and methodical, with her mystery manuscript and revision notes right beside her computer, she still hasn't revised her mystery ending when her writing time is over. Writer #2 and Batter #2 both have direction, but no momentum to carry them to their goals. Getting started successfully requires **both** momentum and direction.

Maintain Your Direction

If you're like Writer #1, someone with enthusiasm for writing and eager to begin, yet prone to scatter your energies, your task will be to gain focus. This is not the same thing as becoming disciplined. I am a very disciplined person, but I often lack the focus necessary to get my writing done. Focus entails blotting out other distractions and staring straight ahead at your goal.

To help myself, I sometimes picture a race horse intent on winning the blanket of flowers. What does he do? Stare at all the other horses? Check out the jockeys? See who's sitting in the stands? No, of course not. He stares straight ahead, focusing on the finish line. Of course, the horse has help—he was given blinders. Writers have to figuratively put on their own blinders when it's time to write. They need to focus on the finish line for that day (e.g., write 1,000 words, revise Chapter 2) and not give attention to other distractions. *But how do we do this?*

Priorities: Urgent or Important?

Without realizing it, we often mistake the important writing tasks for the urgent ones, and vice versa. Yes, it's important that we buy new ink cartridges and study the new market guide, but it's not urgent. It only seems so. What is really urgent is finishing that chapter—otherwise we'll never have anything to print or market at all. Writing is not something to do when everything else is finished, in what little time is left over.

We must work hard to make a switch here. For as long as it takes, for as many days or weeks as needed, tell yourself it's the writing that is urgent and must be done first. **Then do it.** Experts say that doing something 21 days in a row will make it a habit. So challenge yourself to put your writing first—in the "urgent" category—for the next 21 days. Get it done every day, no matter what.

Fire Up!

Suppose instead that you're Writer #2. You already know that your writing is a priority. You even arrange your work on your desk the night before to be ready to write first thing in the morning. You already have focus. Your task is to learn to start with energy. Again, the change that's needed is in the mind.

Picture yourself starting a 100-yard dash, crouched in the starting blocks alongside a dozen other runners. When the gun explodes, how do the runners emerge from the blocks? They appear to have springs in their feet! They leap up and run, lengthening their strides with each step. They don't crawl slowly to their feet, ponder the race track, scan the crowd, or think about what to wear after the race. Instead, they're all moving—and moving fast.

That's the image you must cultivate for yourself. Mentally prepare yourself each night before going to sleep. Picture yourself getting out of bed the next morning with great energy. See yourself moving quickly to the computer, switching it on, putting on your bifocals (if you're like me!), and becoming one with your heroine for the next three or four hours. Then picture the pile of pages written that day. Try this experiment 21 nights in a row, and see if you are then starting with energy that builds momentum.

Get on Base

Even with momentum and direction, you won't hit a home run every day. But you'll be in the game. You'll get on first. The next day you might steal second and race to third. At the end of the week you might even slide into home plate to score.

Getting to Know You . . .

Many of my writing students feel called to write, but they worry that they can't be original, that everything's already been said, and said better than they could ever say it. One of my favorite quotes on this subject comes from C.S. Lewis, famed author of The Chronicles of Narnia and many adult classics: "No one who bothers about originality will ever be original, whereas if you try simply to tell the truth, you will, nine times out of ten, become original without ever having noticed it."

And how do you do this? ***Write what you know.*** Telling the truth, as C.S. Lewis calls it, comes from transforming your personal experiences into helpful and entertaining stories and articles for others. Writing students often say, "But my life has been so unexciting. I've never been anywhere exotic or lived through any natural disasters. I don't have any outstanding talents to share or skills to write about. There's nothing special about me." ***They're dead wrong.***

Take an Inventory
Though we all have tons of things to write about, it can be hard when we're sitting at our

keyboards to think of a single idea. So I've prepared a questionnaire for you, a way to inventory your life experiences. Copy the list, then use a notebook or journal for your answers. (Or try some of the great PC journaling software now available.) Write freely, giving yourself plenty of time to answer each question. Then, as time goes by and you recall other things, go back and fill in sections more extensively.

"Getting to Know All about You . . ."

Over the next weeks and maybe months, take some journaling or free-writing time and answer these questions in depth. This should unearth enough material to last you through the next decade!

l. Where have I traveled? What cities, states, countries? What parks, museums, national landmarks, or historical sites? Where have I been on vacation? How have I traveled (plane, ship, train, bus, car)?

2. What happened in my childhood? Where did I live? What was my home life like? Who was my best friend? My worst enemy? Did I have both parents? Siblings? Grandparents? What was my school experience like? Was my school a one-room building or a large suburban complex? Did I do well in school? What were my favorite (and least favorite) subjects? What did I do for fun? Was I into sports or extracurricular activities? Did I have jobs as a child? What were they? What was the atmosphere like in my home? What were my chores? Did I share a bedroom? Did I have pets? What were my favorite TV shows, books, and games?

3. What relationships have I had in my life? Parents? Siblings? Grandparents, aunts and uncles? Teachers? Husbands/wives? Children and/or stepchildren? Employers? Employees? In-laws? Neighbors? God? Describe the relationships, including problems and challenges. Think of both positive and negative experiences you've had in your lifetime of relationships.

4. What kinds of jobs have I had? List all part-time and full-time jobs, those for pay and those without (include everything from the first childhood job you remember to the present time). List volunteer activities also. What job skills do you possess? What types of people did you work for and work with on each job?

5. How is my health? What illnesses and injuries have I survived? (Go back as far as you can remember.) Have I ever been hospitalized? Has my health affected my life? If so, how? Has someone else's health affected my life?

6. What are my hobbies and interests? Do I play a musical instrument? Am I artistic? Can I sew or do some kind of craft? Am I interested in history and museums? Do I have a collection of something? Do I play sports? Do I have a special skill (flying a plane, calligraphy, raising prize-winning dahlias)? What were my hobbies as a child? What's something I'd like to learn if I had the time?

7. What are my secrets and dreams? What do I want? What do I dream about doing? What would happen if . . . ? What are five things that would make me happy? What are the things that make me angry? What are my favorite quotes, proverbs, poems, Bible verses? What lessons in life have I learned the hard way?

If writer's block strikes as you're "getting to know yourself," try making lists. Use any of the following to stimulate your memories, then be prepared to write fast and furiously! (Whether or not you're planning to write for children, realize that early experiences have shaped your adult perceptions and emotions.)

- smells from childhood
- pets I had
- games I played as a child and as an adult
- restaurants I've eaten in
- places where I felt I belonged
- places where I felt I didn't belong
- places I hid
- places I felt safe
- people, places, and things that I have walked away from
- my very earliest memories
- times in my life I've been very frightened
- books that have changed my life

- fascinating things I have overheard
- secrets I've never told anyone

Write what you know. Get that wealth of information and experience down on paper, and I promise you: **you'll never run out of things to write about!**

What's Your Motivation?

Trouble getting started with your writing? Then you lack sufficient motivation, a strong incentive to get you moving and spur you on. When you can't get started on something—or can't keep going once you manage to begin—turn a magnifying glass on the *why* behind it all.

Motivation: the Key

If you think about experiences in your own life that have tested you, you'll see what I mean. For example, if I'm working out at a gym, it may be a struggle to lift a 50-pound weight. Just driving myself to the gym is a battle. But if that same 50 pounds is a bully pinning my daughter to the ground, I won't have trouble starting toward him. Chances are I won't notice his weight, either, as I fling him aside!

Another example: If I take a night shift job slinging hash so that I can earn money for a new DVD player, I might survive three nights in the greasy spoon. But if slinging hash is the only way I can put three squares on the table for my hungry kids, I'll sling forever. I might not like it much, but I won't have any trouble getting to work.

It's the same with your writing. Do you have trouble getting started? Then examine your motivation. Why do you do what you do?

Celebrity Status

Some write with fame in mind. "I'll show my spouse/mother/boss/third-grade teacher that I'm a success!" You dream of landing on Oprah to discuss the impact your book has had on millions of readers. You imagine book signings and the need for disguising sunglasses to avoid constant pleas for your autograph.

Fun fantasy? Yes. Helpful in getting started with your morning's writing? Not much. Fame is iffy, it's fleeting, it's a dim possibility on the horizon. The writer inside you knows this. Using future fame to motivate you to get started is much like riding a child's rocking horse. It won't get you moving forward.

Riches!

Maybe it's not fame you use to motivate yourself. Maybe it's fortune instead. Big money motivations usually include writing a best-seller. The *best*-case scenario is this: it will take about a year to write the Great American Novel, another year or two to publish it. That's two years bare minimum, and riches only follow if you actually produce a blockbuster. It's hard to motivate yourself to get started writing today in order to earn money two or three years down the road.

But maybe you're motivated by the thought of a small fortune, just enough money to keep from returning to your full-time day job. Although that's a stronger motive, writing for "enough money to get by" can lead to cranking out books and articles just for the check. Don't get me wrong. This can be perfectly good writing (though my own "cranked out" books were neither my best nor most inspired work). Even so, on the days you're just forcing yourself to go through the motions, getting started can be like pulling teeth.

What Works?

If fame and fortune don't motivate you to run to your computer with glee every morning, what would? What motive works every day, rain or shine, in sickness and in health? It's really very simple. It has to do with your gift as a writer—your way with words, your ability to communicate. Is this gift a way to make money, a way to get famous, or a way to share what you've learned with others?

Sharing the Gift

The next time you have trouble getting started on your writing, stop and pose a question. Instead of asking "What's in it for me?" try asking "What's in it for my reader?" How is your piece of writing going to help someone else? This is a key question if you write for children, but it applies to material for adults as well.

Have you learned anything this week or month or year that would benefit others? Maybe you just put your mother in a nursing home. Could you write an article for kids that would take the fright out of visiting grandma in the nursing home and show them what to expect? Or maybe your blended family has struggled through tough times in order to "jell." Is there a story there that might help the millions of kids in the same stepfamily situation?

On a lighter note, did you survive a summer car trip to the mountains with your three kids and two dogs? Could you tell other parents how you coped? When times are tough, does your corny sense of humor come to the rescue? Could you share your wit on a magazine's humor page and brighten someone's day?

20/20 Hindsight

A motive like this ("I know something that could help you") gets the ideas flowing and makes you eager to start writing. As a children's writer, my favorite getting-started trick involves asking myself this question: "What is something I learned over the age of 40 that would benefit a child to know by the age of 15?" That question alone gives me a decade of ideas! Getting started ceases to be a problem. As a writer for adults, I ask myself, "What hard-won bit of wisdom might I share with my friends?"

Helping Hands

The next time you can't get started, examine the motive behind what you're writing. Do you need to change it? Instead of fame and fortune, or even a fun hobby to boost your self-esteem, think about helping someone else through your writing.

Not only will this altered mind-set get you started—it will keep you going.

Increased Creativity

Creativity experts agree that we're all born creative and imaginative but that severe losses in creativity begin in elementary school and continue into adulthood. The statistics are shocking. While a child under 5 tests at **90%** for originality, that figure drops to **20%** by the age of 7 and to **2%** by adulthood! This is scary enough for the general public, but it's frightening in the extreme to people who want to write—to tap into their own creativity—to earn a living.

Psychology texts and websites abound these days with data on the subject of creativity. (If you don't believe me, type "creativity" into your favorite search engine.) When all the technical research is boiled down to everyday language, the bottom line is this: we can all rekindle our sputtering creativity. We can jolt it awake, invigorate it, and enlarge it. This applies to creativity in both our personal and our professional lives.

Sum of Its Parts

Creativity sounds like a single trait, but in fact it's comprised of many parts. Different authors and psychologists call the parts various things, but all agree that to fully develop your dormant creativity, you need to expand in several different areas. Chances are, especially if you're a writer, you already have one or two facets of your creativity well developed. Even so, you may still feel ho-hum and stifled, finding your work becoming repetitious.

If that's the case, identify which of the following four parts of your creativity are under developed. Expand these facets and dramatically raise the overall level of your creativity.

#1 Curiosity

Without an interest in the world around you—what makes things work, what makes people tick, what's happening in other cultures—you have little reason to be creative. Curiosity leads you down unknown, suspenseful paths of learning, "feeding the well" with information and images. Always be willing to keep learning: through books and programs, through classes and art shows, through new experiences. Keep your childlike wonder alive.

#2 Flexible Minds

Being open-minded is essential. Without that, you'll never accept new ideas into your thinking. If you're not open to new ideas, if your mind isn't flexible enough to accept another way of thinking or doing things, you'll tend to repeat the same themes and stories after a while. Don't be a writer who writes the same book over and over. Explore new places, people, and things with an open mind.

#3 Get Out of Your Comfort Zone!

Without a willingness to take some risks, to "do it afraid," you'll never have a career in writing. We take risks when we write honestly, when we submit our manuscripts, when we have something published and reviewed, when we tackle autograph signings and author visits in schools. Some aspects of publishing *aren't* comfortable, like getting rejection slips or having the neighbors shun you after reading your hard-hitting novel. But if you always play it safe and refuse to leave your comfort zone, you'll forfeit new experiences—as well as the courage to write about them.

#4 High Energy Living

Has this ever happened to you? You're curious about something and want to learn about it. You're open-minded and willing to take the risk to write about a touchy subject. Your spirit is willing—but your too, too tired flesh is weak! It happens to us all, for a variety of reasons, but without sufficient energy (both physical and mental) we won't be creative writers. We'll sound tired and bored, and our writing will be an uphill struggle. You need to cultivate the energy that comes from *passion* for your writing. You must really *care* about your subject or story people. The more you love something, the more energy you will have at your disposal for that project.

Test Yourself

Now, take a moment and score yourself (high, medium, low, nonexistent) on each of the four qualities listed above that are required for creativity. Most of us find that we're strong in one or two areas, but very weak in others. **It's not enough to score high in just one or two categories.** For example, even if you have high energy (#4) and you're curious (#1), you won't succeed if you're close-minded (#2) and refuse to take risks (#3).

Score yourself honestly in each area, then focus on the traits where you scored the lowest. Working to improve these low scores will quickly boost your overall creativity. Improving an area where you're already fairly strong won't help as much, so concentrate on your weaker areas.

Working to improve all four facets of your creativity will start you on an upward spiral that will continually gain momentum. Not only will you soon have more creative writing ideas, but your whole life will be lived more creatively. And really, isn't that what we all truly want?

What Are You Thinking?

You turn on your computer, pull up your second chapter to work on, scan your revision notes and then . . . *nothing*. Why? Your mind, seemingly all by itself, slips into wondering how you'll pay for this year's Christmas presents or speculates on the ominous noise your car's been making or worries how to get your toddler to stop throwing tantrums in the grocery store. Your fingers may be poised over the keys, but your mind is a million miles away.

Does this ever happen to you when you're trying to get started? What can you do about it?

Stay in the Present

Experts tell us that in order to be creative, we must stay in the present moment. Only staying focused in the NOW will let you create. Focusing on a past moment (yesterday's tantrum in the store) or a future moment (taking your car to the mechanic) will prevent you from being able to write. This block happens for a number of reasons.

First, if you're worrying about the future or regretting a past event, your emotions consist of anxiety in some form. An anxious state, where your thoughts are churning along with your stomach, is not conducive to writing or any kind of creative thinking.

Second, if you're focused on a past event or a future happening, you're not focused on the writing in front of you. You can stare at the screen, yet not see a word. Generally speaking, our minds can only concentrate on one thing at a time. If we are not actively thinking about the writing task at hand, we won't write.

Third, focusing on worrisome problems and events (whether past or upcoming) causes self-esteem and confidence to take a nose dive. We feel incapable of facing whatever it is we're worried about, and that feeling of incompetence sticks with us. When our self-esteem is shaky, it's very hard to write and edit objectively. Either we can't create at all, or we're unable to cast a constructively critical eye on our work because our weakened ego can't tolerate it.

Mind Control

So what is a writer to do? We all struggle with very real problems in our lives, from the less serious (paying some bills) to the more serious (caring for an elderly parent). *Yet we also want to write.* We are more than our problems. And we love the experience of being able to set aside our concerns, even for a little while, and simply go with the flow of the writing.

Even so, we find it difficult to make our minds behave! We seem to have little control over the direction our thoughts take. However, *to be able to write consistently, this is a skill you absolutely must develop.*

Action Steps

What practical steps can you follow to take back control of your thoughts?

l. Admit you don't have all the answers. When we worry about the future, it's usually when we don't know all the facts. We don't know what the car mechanic will say about the noise or how much the Christmas presents are going to cost. Yet even without all the facts, we recycle the same problem over and over in our minds. This does not create a solution. It just deepens our despair in an obsessive, downward spiral. It creates stress, which makes it even harder to write. The solution?

"Forcing answers, pretending or convincing ourselves that we know what to do, and using habitual thinking all keep us speeded up, *away from the moment* and operating too quickly. Often, an insight will occur only when we fully accept that we don't know what's best," say Richard Carlson and Joseph Bailey, authors of *Slowing Down to the Speed of Life*. So get comfortable with not knowing the answer to everything at all times!

2. Take the pressure off yourself. Have you ever had the experience of trying hard to remember a name, then recalling it just before you fall asleep or when doing something else? It's no accident that you remember something when it's no longer important to you.

We know from experience that our creative thinking process doesn't perform well under pressure. Instead, as we let go and slow down, our free-flowing thinking takes over, all on its own. And it's in that free-flowing thinking that we become the creative writers we dream of being.

3. Try putting the problem and possible solutions on the back burner—just for the next hour or two. Trust that your mind will give you an answer later. The pot on the back burner of your mind requires very little attention, just an occasional stir. You can cook something on the front burner at the same time: your writing. Often, when you go back to check the pot on the back burner, a solution is apparent, cooked up by your relaxed subconscious. The advantage of this method is twofold: (1) you're able to get your writing done, and (2) rather than making a hurried, pressured decision about something, you're able to wait until an answer is clear.

Take Inventory

Anxiety feels so normal to us—regretting past mistakes, reliving past hurts, worrying about future events—that we don't realize how much of our lives it steals from us. We don't realize the energy it drains or how hard it is to be creative.

So the next time you feel blocked, take an inventory of your thoughts. Are you actively thinking about your article or story or book? Are you thinking about character motivation and plot, or a great hook for that article? Or are you living in another time zone, either a past or future moment?

If so, remind yourself that you only have the present moment.

The Here and Now

I urge you to take advantage of the back burner much more often, thus freeing your present moments for your work. If you write at home, you can even do this literally. Set a big cooking pot on the back burner of your stove. Then, on separate slips of paper, write down the worries and regrets that keep you too obsessed to write. Put those pieces of paper in the pot. Put a lid on the pot (don't turn on the burner, though!). Know that the problems are still there, waiting for you when you get done writing if you still want to worry about them.

But in the meantime, enjoy the present moment. Enjoy a whole string of present moments. And use those present moments to tap into your creative flow.

Balanced Truth

Writers tend to go from one extreme to another. One day we write four hours non-stop, emerging glassy-eyed. The next day we meditate, listen to our muse, journal a bit—but write little. We lack balance in our writing lives, balance that allows us to make steady growth as writers and regular progress in our work.

Being balanced means to be evenly distributed—not too much of one thing, and not too much of another. Just as we should eat well-balanced meals to be physically fit, we should also have balanced attitudes to be fit writers. But balanced attitudes can be difficult when the advice we receive is contradictory. Is the truth at one extreme or the other, or somewhere in the middle? How do we find it?

Should we write daily OR only when the muse strikes? Some disciplined writers never skip a day of writing, not even Sundays or holidays or vacations. They are very productive. Others write only when "The Muse is IN." They tend to enjoy writing more, but produce much less.

Should we set strict office hours OR write in snatches of time throughout the day?
Some writers are at their desks by 8 a.m., stopping only for a one-hour lunch break and two l5-minute coffee breaks, just as if punching a time clock. Others (as Julia Cameron recommends in *The Right to Write*) write throughout the day and into the evening, at odd hours whenever the writing can comfortably fit in.

If we write fiction, should we outline thoroughly before writing OR wing it and let the characters tell us the story? Some writers draw up detailed scene summaries for their fiction before attempting a rough draft. Others simply create a character, put him in a tense situation, and go from there, letting the character determine the direction of the story and its plot.

Should we fight for our literary rights OR accept all editorial suggestions and revise without complaint? Some militant writers warn that *no one* can change a word or move a comma in their manuscript without consultation and/or permission in writing. Other equally adamant authors warn writers to revise without complaint because thousands of writers who *will* are ready to take your place.

Should we write longhand drafts to tap our deepest feelings OR always compose at the keyboard? Some writers cling to writing rough drafts and revisions longhand because they feel a deeper connection to their material and believe this produces their best writing. Others scoff at this idea, claiming you'll never make it as a professional, moneymaking writer unless you can compose—*fast*—at the keyboard.

Should we immediately find an agent OR sell "on spec" manuscripts ourselves? Some writers never get an agent, preferring the "do it yourself and maintain total control" approach. They like the freedom of writing on spec and setting their own pace, without pressure. Other writers advise finding a good agent before marketing your first book if you want to get any respect—or money—from publishers.

Should we write for free in the beginning to obtain some publishing credits OR should we be paid for every word we write? Many writers say they started out writing for free until they accumulated clips to send with queries for paying jobs. Others are offended at the idea of writing without pay; they argue that writers are devalued enough already and that writing for free lowers the standard further for all writers.

Clear as Mud

Whew! How can you judge, amidst all the conflicting advice, what is right for you, at this time of your life, with *this* particular project, at *this* point in the process? I personally believe that you need to judge advice on a case-by-case basis. There is no one right answer all the time. In fact, when you rigidly adopt an extreme position on *any* writing issue, you risk eliminating many good solutions to a problem. Being close-minded makes you vulnerable to unnecessary and costly mistakes.

When you have a writing problem, the answer can lie somewhere in the middle, **OR** with either extreme—at different points during the same writing project! You must find your own balance. In the beginning of a writing project, maybe you need to go for a walk and let the muse wander down rabbit trails. Later, as the deadline looms at the end of the same project, you may need to buckle down and adhere to your writing schedule to finish on time.

Flexibility = Balance

At a certain time in your life, one extreme might work for a while, but only for a while. For example, a strictly-adhered-to schedule works great when you have no children, but when the babies arrive, I guarantee you'd better switch to writing in tiny available snippets of time—or you won't accomplish much writing. **ALL** of the advice is right—both extremes—and all of it can be wrong if applied at the wrong time. Strive for balance. Try all the advice, but if it doesn't work for you right now, toss it out and try something else. Be open! If your opinions are set in cement, you will experience much stress when your circumstances change and you can't. See all advice as choices or options, not commandments. Find your own balanced truth.

A Block by Any Other Name . . .

A Rose Is a Rose Is a Rose . . .

If you've been writing any length of time at all, you've experienced writer's block. You may have read articles about it, following different authors' recommendations to blast through your block. Did the solution you tried do the trick? If not, the reason could be that you applied the wrong answer to your problem.

Aspirin or Band-Aid?

If you go to a physician, he doesn't doctor you with a one-medicine-fits-all or one-treatment-fits-all solution. Instead, there are specific treatments for specific ailments: the broken arm gets a cast, the cut gets stitched, the infection gets an antibiotic. Only when you identify the specific ailment can the right treatment be given, or a cure found. The same is true for writer's block.

A Multitude of Sources

Reading an article on writer's block might help you if you happen to stumble across a suggestion that truly corresponds to your problem. But 20 years of writing and 15 years of teaching the craft of writing have led me to believe that there is *no single type* of writer's block.

If you can't identify the origin of your block, treating it is impossible. Have you stopped writing because you can't face any more rejection slips, or your spouse (or a parent) is/was overly critical, or you're disillusioned with having to shape your writing for the market? Are you blocked because you eat or drink too much, sleep too late, or are just plain exhausted from trying to combine writing with earning a living for your family?

Take time to get to know your own blocks. Until you do, until you identify *specific sources of your writer's block*, you won't be able to apply suitable remedies that work.

Possible Causes of Writer's Block

1. Critical childhood voices: **those voices from the past that tell you you're not good enough, you're not creative, you're untalented, or lazy.** They might have originated with parents, grandparents, caretakers, teachers, or siblings. While you may no longer hear actual voices in your head, you've incorporated their views of you somewhere along the way, and they crop up at the worst times for your writing. The resulting feelings of anger and self-doubt produce confusion, sap your motivation, and make you wonder if you should just throw in the towel.

2. *Personality style:* passive or aggressive, outgoing or shy, rigid or flexible, courageous or fearful. An outgoing person may be great at book signings and marketing his work, yet block when it's time to sit down—alone—and write for three hours. The flexible person may have numerous ideas that flow effortlessly and may be able to juggle a number of different projects, yet he may block when it's time to choose just one idea and get to work. The insecure person may write fluently and happily alone, yet block when nearing the end of her story because she's too afraid of rejection to submit a finished product.

Your past may have produced defense mechanisms that can also cause you to block. If you were rejected by parents as a child, you may tend to reject others before they can reject you as an adult. You may quit your critique group, rejecting them before they can reject your work, and end up blocked in your writing. Get to know the quirks—both positive and negative—of your own personality.

3. *Self-criticism:* harsh and self-punishing judgments on our work and marketing efforts. Even when our self-criticism is well founded and accurate, it can defeat and block us before we get started. Self-esteem plummets, courage fails, and we shut off the computer and head for the refrigerator. We're afraid we're deluding ourselves both about the viability of the project we're working on and about our ability to pull it off. This can certainly stop our writing in its tracks.

4. *Marketplace blues:* delays and rejection. After a few months or years of nothing but rejection slips, it can become harder and harder to keep pouring your heart into your work. Sometimes, after numerous near misses and "almost" sales, writers can come to mistrust editors, agents, even the writers in their critique group, wondering if they have hidden agendas. After being rejected enough, the writer may feel unable to face another editorial comment, bad review, or misplaced manuscript, not to mention payment that never arrives and stories that never get scheduled for publication. It's not surprising if he's blocked.

5. *Regular life:* finding time and energy to write while attending to the ongoing demands of life. All the pressures we human beings face—family and financial needs, inner compulsions, leaky faucets, illnesses, difficult bosses—make us feel sometimes that we can't have both a writing life and a regular life, one that includes time for play as well as work. When we're busy writing, we feel guilty about neglecting friends and other interests; yet when we're playing or socializing, we can feel guilty for not writing. This inner push/pull can eventually cause us to block.

6. *Fatigue:* physically worn out. Each step in the creative process requires energy. If you're working a day job to put food on the table, coaching soccer on the weekend, and hosting a dinner party for a friend's anniversary, there may simply be no energy left. You may still want to write, truly want to, but be blocked because for the moment your tank is running on empty.

7. *Environmental blocks:* too much noise and chaos in your surroundings. Writers who can't write at home—who swear they're totally blocked—have been able to write easily and prolifically when transported to a cabin in the mountains or an isolated seaside retreat. Why? They were removed from the noise of city streets, roommates' stereos, toddlers crying, other people's phones, or whatever was keeping them too distracted and on edge to write. Freed from the noise and chaos, surrounded by peace and quiet, these blocked writers often find they're not blocked at all.

8. *Information-specific blocks:* when you can't answer or solve a particular question in your writing. Perhaps it's your first mystery novel, a private eye whodunit. You realize you don't know how it should differ from a police procedural, nor are you sure of the legal limits on a private eye's operations. Or perhaps the 12-year-old hero of your children's book aspires to be an Eagle Scout someday and you don't know just what activities that will entail. You're blocked because you lack specific knowledge. These types of blocks can be taken care of easily, as soon as you identify what it is you need to know.

9. *Skill deficiency block:* when you don't have the practical skill needed to proceed with your work. Perhaps you're blocked in finishing your biography of the first African-American astronaut because you don't know how to acquire permission for the photos you'd like to use. Or maybe you've planned to take your own photos for an article about a local nature reserve; you have the writing all done, yet you're blocked from finishing because you realize you don't really know enough about cameras and lighting and film speeds. These are practical skills you need to acquire before you can unblock.

10. Anxiety and/or depression blocks: nerves, doubts, worries, fears, and panic. This may be the first sign of any kind of block, and the foremost symptom to deal with. Sometimes our worries are realistic. Can we afford to spend time writing stories that might never sell? On the other hand, if we sell a book, will our insecure partner sulk or even walk away? If we write that "coming-of-age" novel, will our parents or siblings recognize themselves in our work and be upset or angry? Anxiety can produce a restless energy that keeps us from being able to sit still long enough to write. On the other hand, depression can leave us too lethargic to get up off the couch and make it to the desk.

A Tailor-Made Solution

Different blocks require different solutions. A few days of peace at a seaside cottage wouldn't help the blocked writer who didn't know how private eyes operate—but it could work wonders for the parent of twins. Taking an assertiveness training/confidence building course won't help the weary postal worker moonlighting to write a historical novel—but it could work miracles for the shy, retiring writer with a drawer full of manuscripts he's afraid to submit.

So take the time to get to know yourself. If you're blocked, find out why. Then outline and implement a step-by-step plan for blasting through your block. Read excellent books on the subject, like *If You Can Talk, You Can Write* by Joel Saltzman, *Bird by Bird* by Anne Lamott, *Deep Writing* by Eric Maisel, and *The Courage to Write* by Ralph Keyes. Help **is** available if you want to break through your personal blocks and create the writing life of your dreams.

Beauty from Ashes

William Shakespeare said, "Give sorrow words." Over the centuries writers have discovered the power in this advice: power to heal emotional wounds, power to write deeply, power to improve their physical health.

Some writers have had difficult, even abusive, childhoods. Caught in a push-pull situation, they feel drawn to writing about it, yet also appalled at the idea. As adults, these writers often suffer from stress-related illnesses and relationship or career problems as a result of stifling those childhood memories. Since both physical and emotional health are affected, sorrow that hasn't been "given words" can also cause a massive writer's block.

Writing = Health

One solution is to meld, or combine, the memories and the writing. Write about the childhood pain or trauma from your adult standpoint. Journal it. Get it out. It may or may not find its way into your published work, but that isn't really the issue. Physical and emotional healing is the issue. *Healing as a person, and healing as a writer.*

Often people advise us to leave the past buried. Why drag it up and write about it? Just move on with your life, they say. Louise De Salvo, Ph.D., author of *Writing As a Way of Healing*, disagrees: "I had a *need* to write. It grew from my pain in living in a difficult household, my sense of difference, my internal, perpetual gloom from the events of my childhood." Pretending the gloom isn't there forces us to wear masks and hide who we are. De Salvo adds, "I didn't know that if you want to write and don't, because you don't feel worthy enough or able enough, ***not*** *writing will eventually begin to erase who you are.*"

Driven to Share

If you read biographies of famous writers you'll note that many authors started to write out of some loss or grief. A desperate need forced them to put words to paper in order to make their experiences real. Up to that point, many suffered from health issues, stress-related diseases, or addictions to alcohol or drugs. They found that expressing the trauma or shock in written words somehow robbed the event of its power to hurt and freed them to move on.

Physical Healing

James W. Pennebaker, Ph.D., has conducted two interesting experiments showing the health benefits of writing about serious issues. In his first experiment, three groups of college students had to write for 15 minutes on four consecutive days. Each student was randomly assigned to a group and told to write about **(1)** something superficial, or **(2)** the facts of a traumatic event, or **(3)** his/her emotions related to a traumatic event. Pennebaker then tracked the number of visits each student made to the university health clinic during the four months after the four days of writing. Those in group # 3 went to the health clinic half as often as the other students. And this was after only four days of writing!

Pennebaker's next study measured the immune function of the writers. He took blood samples before each writing day, after the last day of writing, and again six weeks after writing. The results backed up the first study: People who wrote about their deepest thoughts and feelings surrounding traumatic events they had experienced showed stronger immune function compared with those who wrote about more superficial topics.

Sharing Safely

Our challenge, then, is to learn how to allow our feelings to come up and out as we work, to re-experience them and use them to deepen our writing without the pain crippling us. De Salvo says, "We must enact principles of self-care as we write . . . so that we use our writing to heal ourselves rather than to re-traumatize ourselves." This is very important! The only way this type of writing can help heal is if we can walk away from the work at the end of our writing period and not continue to dwell on it.

So before you try deep (healing) writing, formulate a plan for dealing with the difficult feelings that will come up. Have ideas for distracting yourself when necessary and finding relief from the intensity of this type of writing. Invent rituals both for beginning and for ending your writing periods. One of my own "distracters" when writing this deeply is a "feel-good" movie like *The Sound of Music* or uplifting old family TV shows like *Waltons* re-runs. You will need to discover your own personal rituals for ending a work period and pulling yourself out of your difficult feelings.

Safety Precautions

During your writing period, give yourself permission to write whatever comes up. Even though I later used some of my journal entries in novels, I promised myself before each writing session that *no one* ever had to read what I was writing. This freed me to write honestly.

Promise yourself that if you use the material in fiction later, you'll change and rearrange events so that no one will know it's your own experience. Or promise yourself you'll publish it under a pen name; or that you won't have it published until everyone who might be affected is dead. **Do whatever you need to do to make it safe for the feelings and memories to surface.** That includes writing in a place that can be safe from prying eyes. There are software journals (password protected) that are perfect for this. Notebooks hidden away work just as well.

Self-Soothing

Because deep writing dredges up powerful feelings, you'll need self-soothing techniques *during* your writing sessions too. As you approach your taboo subject, or when painful details emerge during your writing, the temptation will be strong to stop writing and go watch TV, eat chocolate, or sleep—anything to zone out and push the pain back down below conscious level (where it can, of course, continue to fester).

Instead, develop self-soothing behaviors that will allow you to calm your anxieties but not obliterate them. Take a break. Play with the dog. Water your houseplants. Go outside and shoot a few baskets, or jog around the block. Do some deep breathing or yoga stretches. Soothe your inner child, but don't *drug* him or her. When you're calmer, go back to work. Slowly and easily. See what else comes up now and write it down.

Getting started when doing this type of writing can be harder than usual. However, the immense feeling of relief and healing that occurs as you write becomes self-reinforcing. Especially if you've spent months or years repressing and denying your story, you'll note a deep relaxation, a feeling of being spent at the end of the day, that is strangely healing.

Brick by brick, you lighten the load you've carried all these years. You can actually *feel* lighter. Staying in denial requires more energy than facing the truth, which accounts for much of your exhaustion. And once the truth is faced thoroughly, you can heal from it, put it behind you, and move on to a future unhampered by your past.

Sharing Your Experience

You will hear some say that books and stories shouldn't have a message, and there's no room for therapy on the page. That's certainly true if the message is maudlin and/or preachy. On the other hand, if you process pain, learn from it, and remodel your future because of it, you have a right—maybe even an obligation?—to share it.

So often we look back and say, "If only I knew *then* what I know *now*. . . ." Through facing your pain and healing it in your writing you have a chance to write something significant, something that could save another child or adult from going through the pain and isolation you endured.

Studies show that this type of deep writing can significantly improve your physical health—both short-term and long-term. That in itself is enough reason to write about buried issues. But something extraordinary happens to us when sharing our personal hurts also helps heal someone *else's* pain.

Why Does It Take So Long?

Whenever you feel discouraged about your lack of writing success, consider the Chinese bamboo tree. When you plant this tiny shoot, you can expect no growth for up to four years. Even though you water it faithfully, there are no signs that the tree is growing or maturing or will ever amount to anything. **But** if you keep tending the Chinese bamboo seedling all during those somewhat discouraging years, you can expect as much as 80 feet of growth in the fifth year! The tree could never support that rapid growth without a deep root system. Those early growing years, when it appears as if nothing much is happening, are rooting and grounding years.

It is the same with your writing career.

False Expectations

"We may fear failing, but we don't expect to fail," say Sarah Edwards and Paul Edwards, authors of *Secrets of Self-Employment.* "We expect success to be right around the corner." And it's easy to see where we get that idea. TV shows, movies, and soap operas have depicted writers whose first novels were instant best-sellers. Each novel took only a few weeks to write and was sold on the basis of an outline. Each unpublished author had an editor holding his or her hand throughout the writing process (with many face-to-face luncheons to discuss THE NOVEL), then arranging a national book-signing tour.

Oh, *puh-leeze*.

We need to face the fact that a writing career seldom blooms as it does in Hollywood. More often it takes long, lonely years when you're tempted to quit dozens of times. It's at those times we most need to understand about learning and publishing curves and why it takes so long. It seems like such a struggle for us, when it has apparently been easy for others. But it's a mistake to compare *your* publishing curve to other writers, those you know and especially those you read about. You must understand that your particular "success path" will be strictly your own.

Sprinters

I have known a few writers who sold the very first story they wrote. Truly instant success! One was a friend. I had been telling him how hard writing was, how impossible the odds of getting published were—and then he wrote and sold his first story. Was I jealous? You bet! Did I understand why it took me so much longer? No. However, in the long run, I think early success helped set him up for failure. I received 30-plus rejections before I sold my first article. My friend tried a couple more times to sell something, got rejected, and quit. So even though overnight success may look appealing, it doesn't always root and ground you in the writing process, or give you the patience and persistence that will be required later.

People who experience overnight success sometimes have another problem as well. Friends and family expect a series of repeat performances from someone who isn't necessarily sure how she succeeded the first time. The pressure to perform can be intense before sufficient skills have been acquired to support the writing. This pressure easily becomes a block. Quitting often follows shortly. So while overnight success may sound appealing, it comes with its own set of problems.

Tortoises

The tortoise approach is often ultimately the most successful, but it can take so lo-o-o-o-ong to succeed that discouragement can set in. Picture again that Chinese bamboo tree. It is sending roots down for years before its sudden rapid upward growth. If you are writing and studying diligently, you are putting down a writer's roots. It's a critical time, with little to show others for your efforts.

But if you look closely, you can see progress. You may not be making many sales yet, but there is progress in your writing skills, your marketing skills, your networking. You are building a solid base that will support future growth. It will be comfortable, steady growth too; it will add to your life rather than disrupt it. As one Chinese proverb says, "Be not afraid of growing slowly; be afraid only of standing still."

Look Up!

While we may know intellectually that slow growth is more solid, the delays and detours and rejections attack our emotions and strain our patience. After receiving our third rejection in a week, it can be next to impossible to find a good reason to write today or keep up with markets that don't seem to want us.

That's when you need to look up and away. Look up from your desk and your current work and your market guide. Take the long view. Get some perspective. Focus mentally on your goal, your end result, the reason you're plugging away daily at your craft. Each day you write is like taking another step on the journey. You may not *feel* as if you're making progress, but feelings lie. If you're *consistent* (and that's the real key), those steps eventually add up to miles down the writing road.

Each step is important, and each step is taking you down that road. Yes, a few writers will have instant success. They're like boxes of instant brownies—you just add water, pop them into the microwave for 10 minutes, and *voila!* They're ready to eat.

Most of us are the homemade variety, requiring many steps to achieve a tasty result. The time we spend creaming eggs and sugar doesn't feel like we're making brownies. The time we spend sifting flour doesn't, either. Even when all the right ingredients in the right amounts are mixed together, the gooey mess has to go into the oven for 45 minutes. We wait. We drool because we can almost taste success. But provided we didn't skip important steps or quit somewhere along the way, provided we don't walk away from the oven because it's taking too long, eventually we'll have a wonderful pan of homemade chewy brownies.

Better than instant? I think so. Worth waiting for? Definitely! So is your writing career. Learn the skills. Take things in order. Keep at it. Be patient. Get rooted and grounded. Then prepare yourself for surprising growth and success!

Work Habits That Work for You

Unfinished Business

Motivation is what gets you started. Habit is what keeps you going. Without effective work habits, your half-finished novels, plays, and articles won't get completed and won't be published. Plain and simple. But unfinished writing business causes even more serious trouble. It breeds discouragement, lowers self-esteem, and causes a dramatic loss of energy. And this loss of writing energy, sooner or later, could mean the death of your writing dreams.

Sound melodramatic and far-fetched? It's not. This is why.

Three Stages

There are three main phases of any writing project. In **Stage One** we find the idea, do the necessary research, and make the outline. Then we move to **Stage Two**, creating the rough draft of the project. **Stage Three** entails all the revising that takes us to "The End." Productive, efficient work habits carry us from Stage One to the completion of the writing cycle.

Completing a project generates a sense of energy, power, and increased creativity. (Remember the last time you finished an article and mailed it off, or printed out the last chapter of your revised novel to submit? Do you recall the euphoric high, even if you were exhausted?) Although you might take a break from your writing for a few days or weeks following the completion of a project, your mind is free to contemplate the next idea. Even during a break, your brain will be on auto-alert, scanning your environment for ideas, angles, plot twists, and intriguing characters, ready to begin the writing cycle all over again.

On the other hand, without productive writing habits, you'll leave many writing projects abandoned. What's wrong with that?

Draining

Incomplete projects suck your writing energy away. Unfinished business of any kind drains a person. Gazing at a cluttered desk or a sink full of dirty dishes left from last night's party reminds me that I need a nap. Ruminating on an unfinished argument with my teenager makes me want to slump down in front of the TV. Unfinished projects—whether it's the unpacked moving boxes or the half-written novel gathering dust on your desk—drain your energy. You can feel it dribble right out the ends of your typing fingers.

Most of us believe that we begin our days with a limited amount of energy. It's based on our health, how well we slept, our age, and what we ate for breakfast. We use our quota of energy during the day, then must rest to rebuild our depleted stores. This belief is false!

Experiment

Prove it to yourself. Instead of resting the next time you feel lethargic, choose to tackle some unfinished business. Unpack a few more boxes. Finish edging the flower bed you weeded yesterday. Wash your car. Clean off your desk and file that pile of bills and correspondence. Now how do you feel? Even more tired and depleted? No! And here's why: You've actually generated energy by revving up your creative cycle and propelling these unfinished projects toward completion.

Once you get moving, then tromp on your accelerator and really give it some gas. Instead of unpacking at a snail's pace, play some military march music and pick up your tempo. Crank up your speed as you ply your spade. Moving through the completion cycle at a higher velocity increases your energy twofold. Try it and see!

Get Moving!

How does all this apply to your writing? When you're stalled somewhere along the way in the writing cycle (whether it's gathering research for your book on Indian art or doing the final polishing on your whodunit), your energy becomes depleted. The longer you procrastinate, the more tired you get. Unless you get your cycle moving again, eventually you'll pack the novel away in a drawer and stash your research materials in the basement. Despondent, you'll believe you don't have the talent, the perseverance, or the determination to succeed.

What you've really done is unintentionally sabotage yourself by allowing unfinished business to sap your precious writing energy.

Self-Sabotage

We often try to remedy the situation by jerking ourselves up by the bootstraps and setting ambitious goals. As an isolated activity, that just creates more unfinished business. Instead, come up with a more modest, practical goal ("I'll set the alarm earlier and write for an hour before work") and write it down. So far so good—but it's only **Stage One** in creating a new energy cycle.

Stage Two would encompass the first week you experiment with this goal. Some days you'll write brilliantly, some days your dog will join you at dawn's early light and demand a walk, and some days you'll doze off at the keyboard. You'll be tempted to discard your plan. Don't! You'll be dissipating the energy that got you this far.

You need to move to **Stage Three** for completion. Review and revise your morning strategy to accommodate the early rising dog. (Perhaps you can give him a good walk the night before?) Take care of your drowsiness with extra-strong coffee or (even better) going to bed earlier. Revise your morning strategies until the kinks are worked out. This will complete the cycle and give you a writing habit you can count on.

Inventory

Establishing effective writing habits will help you complete the projects you start. When you complete your manuscripts, you experience increased energy, personal power, satisfaction, and pleasure. So next time you experience lethargy in your writing—or in your life—don't take a break right away. Instead take an inventory of unfinished projects. Make a list. Decide which ones you really want to finish. Then overcome your inertia and take the first small step in that direction. Then take another. And another.

You'll be amazed, as you gather speed, how fast your projects are completed and how much energy you have left! Beginning a project with enthusiasm and energy is a fine thing. But although you may grow tired in the second phase, completing a project will once again rejuvenate your enthusiasm and boost your energy—just in time for your next writing project!

Dealing with Distractions

D uring the early stages of a writing project, when you're gathering ideas and deciding on your approach, it's useful to daydream and be unfocused in your thinking. However, there comes a time to focus, to fully concentrate on the work, as if you were putting a beam of sunlight through a magnifying glass to concentrate its power until the paper it touches bursts into flame.

Why Focus?

When you focus, you'll accomplish writing projects in half the time, and your concentrated efforts will produce better work. Focusing also builds momentum and enthusiasm, urging us to move steadily toward finishing our stories, articles, and books.

Being able to focus is critical. As Stephen Covey (author of *The Seven Habits of Highly Effective People*) says, "The main thing is to keep the main thing the main thing."

Getting Sidetracked

What keeps us from focusing? Distractions. They have always been with us. Agatha Christie once said, "I enjoy writing in the desert. There are no distractions such as telephones, theaters, opera houses and gardens." While our modern-day distractions may have changed a bit (e-mails to answer, faxes coming in, the World Series on TV), the result of being sidetracked by them remains the same. We don't finish our writing. We don't study guidelines and mail that manuscript. We don't follow up on marketing tips. If we stall long enough, we may quit altogether.

So how do we deal with things that take us away from our writing? Try adapting the Serenity Prayer for this purpose. "God, grant me the serenity to accept the distractions I cannot change, courage to change the distractions I can, and wisdom to know the difference."

Wisdom to Know

What are some distractions you cannot change or ignore? Sometimes it's a sick child or spouse or a crisis with a friend. Sometimes your boss gives you an overtime assignment with a "now" deadline. There may be a project that needs to be attended to without delay, like your teenager's last-minute college entrance application. This type of interruption or distraction you have little control over. You grin and bear it.

However, we need wisdom to know the difference between the distractions that are unavoidable and those we allow. Chances are, you're your own worst enemy when it comes to distractions that keep you from writing. So take courage! Change what you can in order to focus on your writing.

l. Use an answering machine to screen calls. Better yet, turn the ringer off altogether so you're not tempted to pick up when you hear your best friend's voice. Then return calls at lunch time or when you've finished your daily writing stint.

2. Isolate yourself as much as possible from the traffic flow. I now have my own office, but I've written in family rooms and bedrooms and dens. The family room was the most difficult, with constant interruptions of TV, kids, and doorbells. The more you can shut the door on distractions, the easier you'll find it to focus.

3. Take note of your own personal distractions. The blinds in my office are pulled because I look outside every time a car/garbage truck/motorcycle/UPS truck/bus/delivery truck goes by. I also remove all chocolate from my work space. Even hidden in the back of a drawer, it calls to me while I work and distracts me, whether I stop to eat it or not. Nice weather tempts me to go out for a while, so I don't put on makeup until late in the day. I know I won't show my face in public without it—so I'll stay home and write instead! (For men, not shaving could serve the same purpose.)

4. Leave the mail alone. Reading letters and e-mail can be a major distraction. It interrupts your flow to stop and sort the mail. And if your mail contains rejection letters, bills, and bank statements, it can create an instant slump. So get the snail-mail if you must, but stash it in a basket until the end of the day when you're done writing. The same is true for e-mail. Leave it unopened and unread till late afternoon (unless it's a response from an editor!).

5. *For non-emergencies, make your family wait.* Barter with your family for writing time. When you're finished, you'll make popcorn. When you're finished, you'll play catch. When you're finished, you'll go rent a movie. (Just be sure you actually follow through on your promises!)

6. *Leave home.* If home is too chaotic sometimes, take your work to the library or a park or a cafe, somewhere quiet with no phone and a minimum of distractions.

7. *Organize your work space first.* Arrange your work space before you begin writing, to ensure that you have everything you need. Don't run out of paper halfway through typing your chapter. Keep things within reach. Even finding a new ink cartridge or box of paper clips in your supply closet can distract you. Before you know it, you've spent half an hour rearranging the closet shelves.

8. *Silence can be golden.* Are you as distracted by noise as I am? I run a fan on high speed for white noise, and during school vacations I also use ear plugs. If traffic bothers you—or if you're in a quiet neighborhood where twittering birds distract you—close the windows during your writing time.

9. *Change your schedule.* Get up earlier and write when the world is still asleep. Phones don't ring. Kids don't interrupt. Your spouse is still snoring. (This works equally well if you're a night owl and can write after the world shuts down for the night.)

l0. *Eat healthy meals at regular intervals.* Avoid the distraction of a growling stomach or a hunger headache. If you're always thirsty, keep cold drinks within reach. A mini-refrigerator in your office, filled with bottled water and fresh fruit, can keep you from constantly running to the kitchen.

Focus!

Take time to study yourself, discovering your own favorite distractions. Once in a while we have absolutely no control over interruptions. However, most of the time, we (consciously or not) use distractions to keep us from having to face the work and anxiety of putting words on paper.

The next time you sit down at your keyboard, close your eyes and imagine yourself as that concentrated beam of light focused by the magnifying glass. Then open your eyes, hit the keys, and set the world on fire!

But I Don't Have Time!

The following story will change your perspective on making time to write.

One day an expert in time management was speaking to a group of business students. He set a one-gallon jar on the table in front of him. Then he produced half a dozen fist-sized rocks and carefully placed them, one at a time, into the jar. When the jar was filled to the top and no more rocks would fit inside, he asked, "Is this jar full?"

Everyone in the class said, "Yes."

Then he said, "Really?" He reached under the table and pulled out a bucket of gravel. He dumped some gravel in the jar and shook it, causing bits of gravel to work themselves down into the space between the big rocks. Then he asked the group once more, "Is the jar full?" By this time the class was on to him.

"Probably not," one of them answered.

"Good!" he replied. He reached under the table and brought out a bucket of sand. He dumped sand in the jar and it filled all the spaces left between the rocks and the gravel.

Once more he asked the question, "Is this jar full?"

"No!" the class shouted.

Once again he said, "Good." He grabbed a pitcher of water and poured it in until the jar was filled to the brim. Then he looked at the class and asked, "What is the point of this illustration?"

One eager beaver raised his hand and said, "The point is, no matter how full your schedule is, if you try really hard you can always fit some more things in it!"

"NO," the speaker replied, "that's not the point. The truth this illustration teaches us is: If you don't put the big rocks in first, you'll never get them in at all." [Author unknown]

A BIG Rock

I'm encouraging you to make writing a **BIG** rock in your life. Put it in your jar first, or you may never get it in at all. "But I *really* don't have time to write!" you cry. Think again. Other writers have done it for centuries. Joseph Heller wrote *Catch-22* while working full-time writing advertising copy; T.S. Eliot worked in a bank; Virginia Woolf helped run a printing press. When most of our famous writers started out, none of them had the time to write. But they *made* the time.

Sound impossible in your particular situation? If so, think smaller. I've learned over the years that big, dramatic changes aren't necessary in order to fit writing into your life. It's the smaller, rather easy-to-make changes that can enable you to write and make your dreams a reality. Following are some easy time-saving tips to help you find time to write. These tips are useful for full-time wage earners, stay-at-home moms and dads, the self-employed, and the retired. We *all* need help with this!

Select several tips, implement one today, and another one next week, and another one the next. If you're consistent, little by little, you'll find more time to write.

Time-Saving Tips

Don't allow your TV time to "bleed over" into your writing time. Nowadays, I watch only three daytime TV programs each week. I turn on the TV five minutes before air time, then turn it off when the program is over.

Save current versions of your e-mail address book and bookmark file of favorite websites to a separate disk, or print them out for safekeeping. Avoid a mad scramble if your computer crashes by keeping backups of all important files.

Manage your availability. If you have a cell phone, give the number only to those who must really have it. It's not just a matter of protecting your writing time; you also want to avoid having your "real-life" time eaten up by phone calls when you're out at lunch, running errands, attending a child's ball game, or looking for a good book at the library. Your cell phone should serve *you*—not the rest of the world.

Stop and think from time to time. Analyze where you want to go and see if you're still on that path. We can wander off-track so easily and not even know it. Pay attention! Step back occasionally and ask yourself if you're doing what you need or want to be doing. If not, cut out those time-wasting activities that have crept in.

Take a breather between projects. For years, after finishing each middle-grade novel, I rested briefly over the weekend, then started a new book on Monday. I never allowed myself time off from writing. In retrospect, I believe this was a mistake. My writing got more and more sluggish, more tired-sounding, more repetitive. I finally burned out and wrote nothing for months and months. So now, after completing a big project, I take the time to relax and recharge instead of rushing ahead. Odd though it sounds, taking time to rest between projects can be a great time-saver in the long run.

Don't rush. Hurrying from task to task produces stress and eventually slows us down. Stop rushing through one job to get to the next one. Slowing down will actually help you perform more efficiently.

Don't leave your desk cluttered till Monday morning, with no concrete plan for the coming week. It's a frustrating waste of time to leave scheduling till Monday morning. It's also 10 times harder to get started. Instead, plan your week ahead of time, preferably on

Friday or Saturday before you close up shop for the weekend.

If you're the household chef, try cooking ahead. We all have to eat—but putting dinner on the table can be a daily grind that takes time you'd rather spend writing. Get in the habit of cooking double, then freezing half the main dish so you'll always have an instant meal on hand.

Match your schedule to your biorhythms. If you can only concentrate for an hour at a time and you're most alert in the mornings, then give that first hour of the day to your writing. Get to know your body, and go with its energies as much as possible. One hour of writing during your productive time is worth two or three when you're tired.

Stay on track. One of my biggest time-wasters is my start-and-stop habit. I sit down, outline a story, get up to check on the dog or get a snack, sit back down and type, then check my e-mail, then write some more notes, then . . . You get the picture. Such a waste! Complete jobs you start. Don't start and stop projects with the intention of going back to them later. Stay planted in your chair till you finish.

Either work or take a break. A similar time-waster is half-working, half-resting. I sit down in front of the TV while I skim publishers' guidelines. I'm sorta working, sorta resting. I research my article on the Internet, but take time to read some non-related articles that interest me personally. I think I'm working, but I'm not. I'm wasting time.

If you use the Internet, read a few easy books (like **The Internet for Dummies)** *to learn time-saving techniques for searching, managing e-mail, and creating bookmarks.* Take advantage of software (often free for the download) that will make your work more efficient. I've downloaded free software that reduced the time I spent on some computer-related tasks by as much as 80%.

Get organized! I have two large bulletin boards and a huge tear-off monthly calendar on my wall. My due dates for assignments and projects are posted there, with intermediate and short-term deadlines along the way. Being organized will help you avoid wasted time—time you can then spend writing.

If you have children, get them to share some of the load. My kids were raised on a farm and grew up doing chores, and it still disturbs me how little today's child does at home beyond entertaining himself. Assign kitchen chores to your smaller children, like setting the table or unloading the dishwasher. Older children can cook, mow the lawn, and do their own laundry. Use that freed-up time to write.

Pull your "to-do" list together. Living on a farm taught me to group all my errands in one afternoon each week. Very efficient. Once I moved to town and was just minutes away from the grocery store, library, and mall, I found myself running errands four or five times per week. Such a waste of time! Set aside one afternoon or evening or a weekend morning to do all your errands.

Like Sands through the Hour Glass . . .

Don't let your writing time dribble away. Learn to calculate the time you can spend writing, then use it to the fullest. The better you manage your time, the more writing you'll accomplish and the faster your skills will improve.

Choose one of the small changes above to make today. Then continue making small changes in your daily life, and one day you'll find it easy to put that **BIG** writing rock in the jar first!

No Cheating at the Office

One year I worked part-time at a hectic dental office, typing, filing, and answering the phone. It was soon apparent that I accomplished nearly as much as the full-time employees because I didn't take breaks, didn't hang out in the dental lab and chat, didn't take or make personal phone calls, and didn't snack. I even felt rather smug . . . until I returned to writing at home.

There something dreadful happened to my Protestant work ethic. My productivity dropped sharply, even though I stayed planted at my computer and was busy for two solid hours first thing each morning. Still, I accomplished very little. Less, in fact, than in the days when I typed everything on a manual typewriter. **Why?** I faithfully put in the time, but had little to show for it at the end of the week.

Finally I realized I was kidding myself. I cheated myself out of my writing time by being at the computer, the way my office colleagues had been *at* the office, but not actually working much.

Ways We Cheat

l. Tolerating unnecessary interruptions: When my coworkers at the dental office had wanted to trade gossip, I excused myself with "I leave in an hour, and I've got all this filing to do first." But at home, when a friend showed up uninvited at my front door during my work hours, I nearly always invited her in. (After all, she *knows* I'm at home!) There went my writing time.

I also did not make personal calls at the dental office, but instead jotted a list of calls to make after work hours. Yet often during my writing time, I'd call the vet to schedule my dog's shots or the garbage man to complain that my trash hadn't been picked up *again*. Ten minutes here (on hold) and ten minutes there added up to wasted writing time.

2. Using "time-saving" devices. In my early days of writing, if I struggled with a word or phrase, I looked it up in the dictionary or thesaurus or volume of familiar quotations on my shelf. I found my word or quote in moments, then returned to typing. But when I discovered the wonderful free dictionaries, encyclopedias, newspapers, and virtual libraries on the Internet, I decided to save time and simply click over to look things up online instead. How handy! How quick! Except that it wasn't as fast when my service provider was slow. Moreover, the links on the sites enticed me into further explorations. I found myself "click happy" as I hopped from one famous quote to another (meanwhile forgetting what I'd been looking for in the first place).

3. Handling mail all day long. Years ago, the mail carrier came at three in the afternoon. After my writing time was done, I checked the mail and dealt with it then. I handled mail once: tossed it, answered it, paid it, or read it. Now, when I'm stuck in a passage or feeling the loneliness of the long distance writer, I decide to take just a quick minute to check my e-mail. Need I say more? By the time I've read the mail, discarded the junk, answered a survey, mailed my child an e-card at college, and checked the chat room schedule, nearly an hour has slipped by. At least 98% of the time, there was *nothing* in the e-mail that couldn't wait till I was done writing. On particularly fragmented days, I might check e-mail a dozen times or more, compounding the problem.

4. Playing with computer games and programs. I've never enjoyed computer games, but I know writers who claim they're untangling plot problems while they play Solitaire. Perhaps. But most of them are more expert now at card games than writing. I'm more likely to get sucked into buying programs and e-books I don't need. One year I spent countless hours reading all about web design, how to have an online business, how to get search engine listings, etc. I bought web design software and "paint" programs and mail programs, but I never managed to even create a website for myself, much less run a business. I probably could have written and sold two books in the time I wasted on such endeavors.

5. Organizing. While I find orderliness essential to my writing, I can also use organization to *keep* from writing. I love fiddling with the organizer software that came with my computer. I love the sound effects of the "pages" turning, or the "alarms" that go off to remind me of appointments. I like rearranging my desktop short cuts. Let's see . . . Is it better to group them by subject, or by how often I use them? Perhaps they'd show up better with a yellow background. While I'm changing the wallpaper, I replace my screen saver with one that looks like a brook. At the end of my writing time, my icons are alphabetized, my screen saver sparkles and flows, and my alarm (which plays the theme song from *The Lone Ranger*) reminds me that it's time for lunch. Too bad I didn't get any writing done—but I won't notice, since I spent a whole two hours at the computer.

6. *Eating and drinking.* As long as you're snacking *while* you write, you're still writing, right? Technically, yes. Practically speaking, not necessarily. How much writing time have I lost cleaning cracker crumbs out of my keyboard? Or melted chocolate? And don't even think of what a can of Coke® does to your keyboard. One good spill can wipe out a writing day.

7. *Self-improvement reading.* Within an easy arm's reach is a shelf full of writing books. I can read about organization when my writing thoughts seem scattered. Or I can read that new book on creativity when my thoughts seem dull. Or perhaps I'll just read a chapter or two from this award-winning book on focusing, since my thoughts keep drifting off to other things. I don't leave my desk, I'm immersed in reading *about* writing, but I'm not *writing*. I'm cheating.

Good Old Days

Even though life was duller back in my manual typewriter days, I more easily and more consistently got my writing done. There was nothing else to do while sitting at that keyboard than to write! That doesn't mean we need to throw out our computers or write by hand—but modern-day writers *do* face more challenges. Address them. Figure out a plan. Computers are wonderful machines, but not if their many allurements keep you from writing. **So stop cheating at the office. Remember: writers *write*.**

Recovering from Speed Sickness

Does the following scenario make you suspect I've been peering over your shoulder?

The Modern Writer

You're nearing the end of writing a fantasy novel when you read in a marketing newsletter that So-and-So Editor has moved to Such-and-Such Publisher and wants nonfiction books on bugs ***now***. You feel pressured to drop the novel and whip up a ladybug-book outline. Tension builds as you get sidetracked in the research. Several days later, the nonfiction proposal is almost ready, but you feel guilty about not completing the fantasy novel, since an editor kindly said "Send it!" two months ago.

On Monday morning you resolve to clear your desk of everything, finish that novel and mail it off, then get back to the bug book. The pressure mounts. (You just *know* Editor So-and-So is going to snap up an inferior bug book proposal before yours gets there!) No matter what you work on, you feel as if you need to be working on something else.

Then your critique group leader e-mails an urgent notice describing a short story contest. The prize *does* look good. So you drop the novel and the bug book, dig through your files for any rejected manuscripts you could spruce up and submit, killing yet another writing day. You find something, but the rewriting of the insipid story takes longer than if you'd started from scratch—which you finally decide to do, losing another writing day.

The pressure gives you a headache, so you down a couple of aspirin and take a break to read a chapter from that *Get Organized Now!* book you bought. You read until you discover the book is missing the middle 30 pages. You locate the online used bookstore that sold you the book so it can be returned; *where* is that customer service e-mail link? By the time you find it, dig out your account number, explain the problem, and pack up the book to ship back, another writing day is lost.

And the Point Being?

The end of the week arrives. Your novel hasn't progressed. The ladybug book proposal isn't finished—and you don't want to finish it because, after all, you really aren't interested in bugs of any kind. The story for the contest stinks and reminds you that you never did like writing short stories. You worked at top speed during every writing hour during the week. You ended up further *behind*, not ahead, and frustrated enough to cry. You determine to work harder and faster the next week. And so the cycle repeats.

Instead, let me urge you to **slow down . . . and get more done.**

Simplify

I love the fact that we have so many choices and options. Yet the writers I know are more and more stressed these days by time pressure and hurry-hurry speed sickness. You can have too *many* choices, resulting in bad habits that create so much pressure you don't accomplish anything.

It doesn't have to be this way. These are not inborn, natural reactions; they are learned behavior. You've probably reacted to circumstances this way for years, and now it's a habit. But you can work to change the habits that hurt you. You can study your life and your personality, then choose a strategy that works for you.

> Your methods of getting yourself out of the time pressure trap may include many different ploys. You should try the suggestions of others, but in the end you'll probably need to invent your own rules, based on an honest monitoring of your progress to see if what you're doing really works. Take the time to reclaim your life!

Simplify your schedule. Don't answer e-mail all day long. Don't pay bills and answer letters as they arrive. Set aside one or two specific times per day for the e-mail, and one time per week for the snail-mail. Dealing with it at one sitting is much more efficient and makes you less frazzled. Don't feel pressured to answer every e-mail or letter. Set them aside— maybe even make a special file folder or wicker basket for the week's mail. Put "answer mail" on your schedule and know that you will attend to it all at that one specific time.

Made to Order

Different personalities need different working styles. You may need to choose one project and work to complete it before starting another one. While some people love jumping around and are quite productive that way, others (who prefer quieter, more methodical ways of working) find it stressful. They need to slow down, choose one project, and simply set others aside till they complete this one.

Those other ideas can go in a box or file folder, to be sifted through when this one is completed. 99.9% of the time it won't matter if we mail that new proposal out today or in three days. It will likely sit on an editor's desk for months, and breaking our necks to get it out ASAP will just drive us nuts. Slow down!

Keep things within easy reach when you're working. This includes the research notes you need, the cough drops, the bottle of water, your sweatshirt if you get cold, and the caller ID box to check when the phone rings. If you have to physically jump up and down all the time (running to the kitchen for a glass of water, to the dining table for your spread-out notes, to the bedroom for a sweatshirt) your mind will be fragmented. You'll have to "start writing" over and over instead of starting just once and smoothly continuing.

So I challenge you to think about your concept of time. Shake the pressure and the tyranny and get into your own natural rhythms. Relax. Slow down. And yes, you'll get **more** done!

Boosting Productivity

I t seems almost too obvious to state, but in order to sell more and make more money at your freelance writing, you have to write more. Plain and simple, you say? Yes. An often overlooked strategy? Surprisingly, that's a "yes" too. Even veteran writers miss the obvious sometimes.

Cash Flow Crunch

Recently I faced several major expenditures above and beyond the normal household expenses. Two children needed more college money, one needed wedding money, one needed braces and elective surgery. I didn't require extra income immediately, but huge sums would be due over the course of the coming year.

For about three days, my brain was in Deep Freeze Mode. I couldn't imagine how a freelance writer could possibly make more money without sacrificing time with family (which I consider a priority) or sleep (which I needed to handle a chronic pain problem). I was already working to full capacity, wasn't I?

Or was I?

A Puzzle

Since I couldn't boost productivity by working longer hours, I would have to make better use of the hours I already worked. For some mysterious reason I wasn't accomplishing much more with my kids in school all day than I had when they were babies and toddlers.

> *Something was wrong with this picture!*

Plug the Leaks!

To find the problem, I cast a critical eye on my usual working day. True, I got up early, before the children, but I spent a large amount of time sipping hot chocolate, writing in my journal, doing a few exercises, chatting with the kids, dressing while watching the morning news, then walking the dog for 45 minutes. I was up for a full three hours before I ever sat down at my computer.

I noticed that my "summer-only" TV habit (acquired while I was recuperating from surgery) had extended long after school started in the fall and I was perfectly healthy. Oh, I folded laundry or started supper while I watched my soaps, but there was no denying that this was a waste of quiet, potentially productive hours.

In addition, I'd continued the summer habit of answering the phone instead of letting the answering machine get it. I took about 60 minutes of calls during the day that I could have waited till after five to return—if at all. I was also in the habit of leafing through the mail when it arrived at noon, paying bills that came, reading through the video and book club ads before tossing them. Another half hour down the drain. I often drove to the post office and bank after lunch instead of waiting till late in the day, when the kids were home and I couldn't write anyway. Another quiet half hour of writing time lost.

Just taking an honest look at my day told me where to plug the leaks. I didn't need to write evenings and weekends to make more money. I simply needed to make good use of the time I was already blessed with during the day.

Tips That Stand the Test of Time

l. Set schedules and priorities. Set aside regular daily and weekly times for writing. Use idle snatches of time—even 10 or 15 minutes—to jot down notes, create titles and character sketches, or work on outlines (instead of leafing through a magazine or watching the news for the second time that day).

2. Get organized. Put all materials for each story or article in a separate folder, keeping records of submissions on the outside of the folder. It's time-saving and efficient. A separate box or basket for each book project works well too. Don't waste precious writing time hunting for materials.

3. *Use your non-writing time to pre-think.* Whether you're mowing the lawn, commuting to work, or sorting the laundry, use your non-writing time to think through plot problems, mentally compose your article's hook, or rehearse realistic-sounding dialogue. Then, when you're able to get to the keyboard, you'll make the most productive use of your time.

4. *Try a new writing time.* Once I read that "real writers" got up before their families and wrote at five a.m. I tried that, and froze in the winter and dozed off in the warm summer months. When my children were small, I tried a writing time that fit me—during nap times and *Sesame Street*—and my productivity and the quality of my writing tripled.

5. *Try new surroundings.* If your present writing place isn't working for you, change it. Can't produce even a limerick at the dining room table or the family room with the TV on? Try a quiet corner of your bedroom or basement instead. Be creative. Get rid of the notion that "real writers" write in fancy offices. *Real* writers write wherever they can.

6. *Stay busy.* Sounds obvious, but many writers ignore it. Don't finish a story or article, mail it to a publisher, then rest on your laurels while you await word of its fate. What a waste of time! What lost momentum! Have a new project to work on immediately and get going.

7. *Set goals within goals.* It's difficult to get going and keep going on a writing project that appears overwhelming. Break it down. Slice the project into pieces you can swallow at one sitting. For every writing project I'm working on, I have a typed list of tiny steps to take from beginning to end. I focus on the next step to take, feel very productive when I can cross it off the list, then start the next step. This step-by-step method actually seems to shrink large writing projects, making them less imposing.

8. *Keep a daily log of writing accomplishments.* Make a note of every query, outline, article, story, and book chapter written, every dreaded phone call made, every research trail followed. Rereading previous pages gives you a great overview of your work habits with an eye toward improvement. You may either discover that you're much more productive than you thought—or that you're not actually accomplishing nearly as much as you assumed. A daily log doesn't lie!

9. *Set deadlines.* If an editor hasn't set a deadline for you, set one for yourself. Put that deadline in big red letters at the top of your step-by-step goal sheet. A deadline will spur you to complete the project.

More Productivity Equals More Income

It's all pretty simple. If you want to make more money writing, you probably have to write more. You needn't give up your family and outside interests to do it, either. Instead, train yourself to capture the minutes and hours, and your writing days will take care of themselves.

Time Pressure? Be Early!

At least five times a week, a writer complains to me about needing to "get caught up." The catching up may involve studying the markets, getting a query or manuscript in the mail, meeting a book deadline, or transcribing an interview. I almost never hear from people who consider themselves "caught up." I don't believe I've *ever* heard from a writer who was working ahead. And yet, according to time management expert Don Aslett, that's what we should be striving for.

> "The simple, inexpensive principle of being early will single-handedly, automatically, for no cost and little effort, prevent about 80% of your 'time management' and personal and organizational problems," Aslett claims in his book, *How to Have a 48-Hour Day.*

Be Early?

Most of us are thrilled to get to the end of a day or week and feel caught up, that we've met our goals or quotas and can relax. But if we want to do our best writing, we need to work *ahead*, not behind. This gives us a time cushion, and if we encounter problems, we have built-in time to handle them. Otherwise, in an already over-full schedule, emergencies cost more time and money and frustration to fix, putting us further behind.

I did some checking with writers I know. Sure enough, at least 90% of people I interviewed keep a backlog list of things that should be done. These are projects to dig into if they ever get caught up with their daily list of things to do. But since they are chronically behind (like football teams that find themselves 30 points behind at half-time), they play a stressful game of "catch up" and rarely have time or energy to tackle the backlog.

Go-Getters

High-producing writers don't have backlogs. They maintain a frontlog, a list of things to do ahead. The log includes projects due several months away, speeches to be made, trips to be taken, items to budget for. The list is visible (like my new one on a typed 3" X 5" card taped to my computer) so that it stays in the forefront of my mind. "When you're always working ahead of yourself," Aslett says, "pushing things ahead of you rather than pulling them along behind you, you have twice the control." You also need half the energy because there's no time pressure involved.

Eliminate the Time Pressure

(1) Create a frontlog. Make a list of your upcoming projects and deadlines. (Right now mine

includes writing a speech and researching two books.) Keep the list in front of you. Keep materials pertaining to these tasks with you. (For example, because I had paper on hand, I worked on my speech while waiting at jury duty.) I keep a file folder for the speech and drop in quotes and articles I come across and print out. I chip away at the projects when I have a few moments here and there, with no pressure at all because I'm working ahead. Gradually the jobs get crossed off the list. (Add new ones as you commit to future projects or events.) When it was time to write the speech, my material was all there.

(2) Do things EARLY in the day. I decided to rearrange my schedule. I was using too much energy on my morning aerobics. "For me," says Aslett, "the morning hours will always out-produce the evening hours 3 to 1. I do all my finely tuned mental stuff such as writing in the wee morning hours." He left the office-type stuff (like filing) for afternoons, and the physical labor (including exercise) for the evenings. Made sense! I tried it, walking the dog for an hour in the evening instead. I was astonished at the increased writing output in the morning.

(3) Have "frontlines" instead of deadlines. I stopped dead in my tracks when I read the following statement: "Deadlines are a crutch for the weak-willed and unmotivated," Aslett says. "Deadlines eliminate all the joy of accomplishment as you're working for the deadline, not the completion of the project or task." This takes a major mental adjustment. I always believed deadlines were invented and kept by strong-willed, motivated people!

But as I pondered Aslett's statement, I realized it contained a large grain of truth.

Having tight deadlines (either because I accepted an unrealistic due date from a publisher or because I procrastinated so long that it became tight) took the joy out of writing. A motivated writer *wouldn't* wait till the last minute to finish a project. I needed to demand reasonable deadlines from publishers, and then get to work immediately, rather than creating my own time crunch and pressure.

People who live by deadlines tend to start projects a day late rather than a day early. This cuts them out of other opportunities that might come along because they have no cushion of time. They have a deadline to meet! (A project that will no doubt be delivered by Federal Express or overnight mail.)

(4) Fix things early. Are you like me? I ignore slow leaks in tires (which are easy to fix) and have blow-outs later and pay for towing costs. I hear strange noises clunking in my computer and hope they will go away—which they eventually do, along with all my saved files. I keep reminding myself that my ink cartridge is low, but I don't buy a spare till I run out (halfway through printing a long manuscript that is—you guessed it!—due at the post office in 20 minutes for Overnight Express in order to meet a deadline). If you ever want to have a 48-hour day, fix things, buy things, and tend to things early, when you first spot the problem. It will save you time, money, and aggravation.

So next January 1, if you need a terrific New Year's resolution, try this one on for size. Resolve to work ahead, finish early, use a frontlog, and (as a wonderful byproduct) triple the enjoyment of your writing experience!

Divide and Conquer

Although my book deadline was just a week away, and although I sat in front of my computer every day for hours, very little was being written. My mind wandered from my aching back (why couldn't my teenager shovel snow for me?) to my daughter's new boyfriend (was he as shifty as he looked?) to my bank account (what had my husband done with the money I had saved?). Every 15 minutes, I started over on Chapter Six. By the end of another work day, I'd accomplished little. Why? I lacked focus. Worrisome thoughts about my family kept intruding.

Just that morning I had read in Andrew J. DuBrin's book *Getting It Done* that self-disciplined people could divide their lives into compartments, then concentrate on just one part at a time. That certainly did not describe me! Actually, this came as a bit of a shock. I considered myself very self-disciplined. Some people even called me driven! But lately I certainly was not keeping the various parts of my life separated. There was definite bleed-over.

What now?

If you can't learn to compartmentalize, your writing will suffer. Brooding over the argument with your partner or your mother's illness while trying to work will result in mediocre writing (if you get any done at all) without changing anything about the argument or about your mother's health. That in turn may make the non-writing problems loom even larger. ("How can I take time tonight to go visit Mom when I got so little writing done? I'll never make this deadline if I don't keep working.") Failing to compartmentalize makes all areas of your life suffer, not just the writing.

Interference and "bleeding over" into your writing occur most often when a problem or crisis happens in a major area of your life—something affecting your spouse and children, your day job, your health. Reactions vary, but yours will probably include at least some of the following:
- Physical symptoms: upset stomach, increased heartbeat and breathing rate, chest pain and tightness, muscle aches and pains.
- Mental symptoms: difficulty concentrating, forgetfulness, careless mistakes.
- Emotional symptoms: tension, short temper, mental and emotional fatigue.
- Behavioral symptoms: restlessness, constant snacking, agitation.

When you're writing—or trying to—be alert for those signs. They're signals that your mind has wandered and that personal problems have invaded your work. We all have our individual stress symptoms. Mine include restlessness and an upset stomach; a more passive person might experience forgetfulness and muscle aches. Learn your own particular signs to watch for.

Once you realize that your thoughts have leaked and mixed together, how do you get your focus back on your writing? You learn to put things in individual compartments. How? By separating the issues. ***Divide and conquer.***

Nuts and Bolts: How to Compartmentalize

(1) Regain Perspective: First, realize that it's your *perception* of the troublesome event and not the event itself that has you upset. Odd as it sounds, the stress that is keeping you from writing usually doesn't stem from the bothersome event itself. It's over. That event can be days or weeks or years in the past. Instead, you're reacting mentally and emotionally to your *interpretation* and constant replay of the event.

Continuing to react as if the event had just happened is counter-productive at best, and usually very harmful. Yes, the situation may still have to be dealt with, but sometimes just realizing the event itself is ***over*** does a lot to decrease your agitation.

You can then move into the more helpful "How do I choose to respond to this event?" mode. That type of action-oriented thinking makes it easier to compartmentalize. You can consciously set aside a specific time to deal productively with the problem (whether that involves seeing a counselor, calling a friend, writing a letter—whatever steps are necessary).

(2) Thought-stopping: Mentally or verbally say "Stop it!" when you realize that your thoughts have drifted off again. Then deliberately refocus on the writing at hand. Quietly but emphatically repeat your "stop it!" phrase whenever your anxiety-producing thought occurs again. When you first try to eradicate a troublesome thought, you may need to do a conscious thought-stopping 50 times in one day.

It's important to act quickly when negative or irrational or fearful thoughts surface. This isn't easy, especially for those of us who are worriers, but you can learn to do it. Rather than mentally play with the worries, resist them at their onset. The sooner you practice thought-stopping after you realize you're distracted, the easier it will be to refocus and the less frequently you'll be troubled by this problem.

(3) Focus Visually: When you realize that your thoughts have strayed again to your negative bank balance or your daughter's oddball boyfriend, stare at something in your field of vision until you regain your focus. You can stare at the last line you wrote, or you can choose an image expressly for this purpose. (I use a tiny picture taped to the edge of my computer screen of Snoopy typing on top of his dog house; the bubble over his head says, "It's exciting when you've written something that you know is good!") Stare at your chosen image/object until thoughts of your bank balance and the boyfriend retreat into the recesses of your mind, to be dealt with later.

(4) Verbal Self-Talk: Give yourself firm directions. Say them out loud several times. Experiment till you find what works for you. Some writers berate themselves aloud if they find themselves procrastinating. I personally find positive statements of intent more helpful, like "For the next hour, I will think only of my writing. I give myself permission to put my anger at my spouse (or whatever is bothering me) on the back burner until that time." Tell yourself that you can pick that worry back up in an hour. (By then, you may not want to!)

Obviously, if you're in the middle of a true crisis demanding immediate action, you can't ignore it. But most of us spend time worrying or fretting to no purpose—spinning our wheels instead of doing anything concrete to solve the problem. That's simply wasted time that would be better spent writing.

So the next time you find yourself staring blankly at your computer screen, pay attention to your thoughts. Have they wandered into fretting and stewing? Then stop them. Redirect them. **Compartmentalize.** *Divide and conquer!*

Too Much Time?

I sold my first book two weeks before my youngest daughter was born. She joined a brother (7) and two sisters (5 and 2). My first five or six middle-grade novels were written with babies and toddlers underfoot, and I was also teaching at the time. So when I spoke at my first writers' conference and then lunched with a full-time writer whose children were grown and married, I had to bite my tongue **HARD** when she voiced her frustration at getting so little writing done.

My thoughts were downright nasty, although I smiled through gritted teeth. *YOU can't get any writing done?* I silently fumed. *You have all day to write with no interruptions! If I had that much time, I'd write the Great American Novel.*

Humble Pie

Experience can be humbling. It's now eighteen years later, my "baby" is off to college, and I haven't had to juggle writing and small children for years. So am I more prolific than ever? Ashamed and embarrassed, I have to say "no." In fact, I sound suspiciously like that older woman from my first writers' conference. Because the truth is: I now have tons of time to write without major distractions, and I struggle more to write these days than when the children were small. This unexpected twist of fate truly shocks me!

According to Parkinson's Law, a project will tend to fill all the time allotted for it. Time and experience have proven this true. When my children were babies, I had one (and occasionally two) precious hours per day for my writing. I knew how much I could reasonably expect to write in that time, and the minute the kids' tousled heads hit their pillows at nap time, I started typing. And nine times out of ten, my daily goal was met. Today, I still get about two hours of writing done per day—when I'm lucky. However—and this is the mysterious part—that two hours somehow fills up the whole day.

A Snail's Pace

It was taking hours for me to get started, after answering personal e-mails, watering my flowers, and walking the dog for an hour. By the time I was set to write, I was hungry because it was nearly lunch time. Whereas lunch once consisted of half a peanut butter sandwich snarfed down with the kids, it was now more elaborate, eaten in front of an hour-long soap opera (another embarrassing habit I acquired).

Since I was so relaxed by the end of the soap, I needed another ritual after lunch to get started *again*. I'd phone my daughter, or sort through the mail that arrived, read an article or two from a new magazine, and then maybe take a nap (especially if my lunch was heavy on sugar, which made me drowsy). It could have been as late as 2:30 or 3:00 before I was back at work. By the time I checked my e-mail again (following those tantalizing links that promise you megabucks for simply surfing the Net), it could have been nearly 4:00. Then, in a burst of energy, I'd get my second hour of writing done before it was time to cook supper. Of course with all this dinking around, I'd still have most of my web editing responsibilities to attend to after supper, leaving me working until 9, with no evening leisure time.

After several months of this ridiculous schedule, I finally admitted I had a problem. I was at the keyboard off and on all day, from 9 a.m. to 9 p.m., and getting very little writing done.

Solution

Then one day, while reading one of my many e-mail newsletters, I came across an article by Dr. Donald E. Wetmore called "The Top Five Best Time Management Practices." One of his suggestions, which I recoiled from at first, was to "overload your days." But his explanation made sense, at least for this season of my life. He advised:

"If we give ourselves one thing to do during the day, it will take us all day. If we give ourselves two things to do during the day, we get them both done. If we give ourselves twelve things to do, we may not get twelve done, but we may get eight done. Having a lot to do in a day creates a healthy sense of pressure on us to get focused and get it done. We almost automatically become better time managers, less likely to suffer interruptions, not waste time in meetings, etc. by having a lot to do."

I was skeptical. For one thing, I'd fought my Type A workaholic tendencies for years. It had caused major health problems. Surely overloading my day was a step backwards and couldn't be a good idea. Or could it?

When I was honest with myself, I had to admit that workaholism was no longer an issue. It had been a decade since I'd juggled four kids and two jobs, dashing madly from one activity to the next from sunup to sundown. In fact, between the kids growing up and mid-life creeping over me, I had slowed down a lot. To a crawl some days. I had *become* that woman from so long ago, the one I had absolutely no sympathy for.

Experiment

I figured it couldn't hurt to try Dr. Wetmore's advice. I was fed up with working every evening to make up for my snail's pace during the day. So one night before I went to bed, I sat down at my desk and wrote out a list of nine tasks to "overload" the next day. Then I promised myself I'd be at my desk at nine sharp. Guess what happened? Without hurrying or being frazzled, I accomplished all nine items—and I still took my hour for lunch.

Dr. Wetmore was right. That "healthy sense of pressure" kept me focused during the day. When the phone rang and my caller ID identified my best friend, I glanced at my "To Do" list, then let the answering machine pick up. When three newsletters and an e-mail from my editor arrived in my Inbox, I glanced at my "To Do" list again, answered the editor, and left the newsletters for after work hours. Small decisions like this throughout the day enabled me to get a full day's work done with no hurry, no hassle. Actually I felt energized at the end of my productive day, where before I'd felt exhausted after accomplishing little.

File for Later

All you young moms and dads with demanding tasks every waking moment will meet this advice with a snort. ***I'll** never sit around wasting time when I have the freedom to write,* you think. That's what I always said, too. A word to the wise: never say never! Instead, tuck this advice away for a decade or two, just in case (like me) you transform from a hare—to a tortoise!

Journal through the Summer

For a variety of reasons, writers often have difficulty writing during the summer. Your children may be out of school and underfoot, or you may have a house full of company. You may have trips and vacations planned. Warm weather may entice you onto the beach or golf course. Whatever the cause, you're thrown out of your writing routine. Sometimes you stop writing altogether and lose your momentum. One solution? Journal through your summer.

Journaling is a hobby with many advantages. It's inexpensive. A cheap spiral notebook will work just fine. Your journal is always available, and all you need in the way of equipment is a pen. Journaling can be done at any time of day, in any type of weather, for as long (or short) a time as you desire.

Are We Having Fun Yet?

Journaling is meant to be fun. Don't put expectations on yourself during journaling time. Forget about your performance, and don't critique yourself. Relax. Let go. Writers need a place to write where "enjoyment" is the only requirement. Ask yourself frequently, "Am I having fun?" If not, loosen up. Write from your gut. Be totally honest. If you can relax and have fun, you'll eventually discover the natural writing "voice" within you. You won't have to try. Your unique voice will simply flow out onto the page.

Journal the Joys

Journaling during the summer has many advantages. If you're traveling, it can provide written snapshots of the people you see, the places you go, and the things you do. (Back home, these descriptions easily translate into nonfiction ideas or into characters, settings, and plots for your stories.) If a special event is scheduled—a wedding or the birth of a grandchild—journaling is ideal for capturing those special, once-in-a-lifetime feelings. If you're surrounded by active children, journaling provides a practical and convenient way to capture creative ideas on the run, since a useful journal entry need take no more than 10-15 minutes.

Journal the Blues

Journaling can also be beneficial in helping you work through *un*pleasant feelings that summertime sometimes produces. Perhaps your cross to bear is your in-laws' yearly two-week visit. Journal beforehand, journal during the visit, and journal afterwards.

Before they arrive, write about your feelings of dread. Remember (on paper) the past visits. Describe how you hope this visit will go, then brainstorm ideas that can make that dream a reality. During their visit (perhaps late at night) journal your frustrations, failures—and successes! Use the journal for a dumping ground of negative feelings. (Be sure to hide the notebook!) After they return home, a journal can be used to process the visit. How did it go? What did you learn? What would you do differently next time? Was there improvement? (Later, these notes could become a how-to article on structuring a successful in-law visit.)

Journaling Dreams

Journal through your summer by exploring your dreams and daydreams. Give yourself free rein to imagine the kind of life you'd love to live. No restrictions. Journal about where you'd like to live, things you'd like to experience, new foods you'd like to eat, different hobbies you'd like to try. Let your mind wander off onto all sorts of delightful tangents, then capture those daydreams in a journal.

You'll begin to notice common threads. Perhaps you'll discover all your daydreams center around creating more simplicity in your life. Perhaps they express a need for more adventure. Perhaps they'll uncover a buried dream or goal from long ago. Slow down, and take the time to get to know yourself again.

Journaling Creativity

Use a summer journal to explore more facets of your creativity. Perhaps you've written and published numerous nonfiction pieces. In your journal, experiment with poetry. Draw a picture. Write an essay or a fairy tale. Create some song lyrics. Write a fantasy story if you've always written modern-day thrillers. You may be surprised to uncover hidden talents in areas you never explored before.

Use a summer journal to take snapshots. In addition to using a camera, use your journal. After you snap a picture of Grandma reading to your son, write a journal entry describing the scene. Be liberal with sensory descriptions, and use *all* your senses. Describe the lilt in Grandma's voice, the tattered childhood book, the creaking of the rocking chair, your son's terrycloth sleeper, how he curls into her bent arm. Capture memories with the sensations of the moment. I intend to keep a journal when I visit my daughter at the birth of her baby. I'll take a million pictures, but I also want a written account of those first days and weeks of the baby's life. It will contain treasured memories to enjoy myself and share with others.

If this summer's crowded calendar has you throwing up your hands and walking away from your computer for a season, take heart. Your writing isn't over for the summer. Instead, switch gears. Buy a notebook and pen, and this year journal your way through your summer.

Money and Other Practical Matters

A New Relationship with Money

F reelance writers quickly find that in order to succeed, they have to develop a new relationship with money. When we have a weekly paycheck, we "earn in order to spend." As self-employed freelancers, we need at times to shift to a "spend to earn" policy whereby money must **sometimes** go *out* before it comes *in*. To put it another way, you may have to support your writing habit before it can support you.

Impossible!

I can already hear many of you crying out, "But I don't have the money for that! I can't buy a computer!" Or "I can't even afford stamps and envelopes." Or "I spent all my money setting up an office, so I can't order stationery or business cards." It's a common reaction from most of us, one I had to consciously fight—and still have to fight.

I'm the proverbial person who saves for a rainy day. I like to have everything planned for, and I never buy cars unless I can pay cash. I was raised on the family motto that "if you don't have the money, you don't buy it." It's a wonderful philosophy, and it's enabled me to live on a freelancer's shoestring budget more times than I can count. It's solid teaching to pass along to your children, too, especially in this day of easy credit that urges you to "buy now, pay later."

Shifting Sands

However, if you want to succeed as a home-based business person—and that's what freelance writers are—you need to make a mental shift in certain areas. When you're on your own, without a paycheck, you must learn to think of money in different terms. You're no longer on a fixed income. Instead, you must adjust to some different freelance realities.

(1) You must support your business before it will support you. Keep your day job long enough to finance your start-up costs. If you don't have a job, just be more creative. When I wanted to take a writing course 20 years ago, I had three small children. My husband correctly guessed that there was no extra money in the budget for this course. But he also said I could sign up if I could figure out where to trim the budget.

So I did. I already made the kids' clothes and we rarely ate out, so the grocery budget was the only "elastic" fund. I began baking all our bread, plus making homemade yogurt and homemade jam. We drank powdered milk—bless the kids' hearts!—and no one complained when the meat in the stew was almost nonexistent among the homegrown vegetables. (Believe it or not, family members still recall those as their best meals!) It was a lot of work, but I managed. With the money I saved, I took the course and sold three of my assignments, which launched my writing career.

I'm not suggesting you should all become earth mothers or fathers, growing your own food and weaving your own cloth. Everyone's situation is different. You might support your writing habit by baby-sitting several evenings a week or painting someone's house or doing yard work. (If these sound like teenage odd jobs from your past, look around you—how many teens these days are available for such chores?) However you accomplish it, find a way to support your writing habit financially until it can support you.

(2) You have to spend money to make money. Countless editors have remarked that handwritten submissions on personal stationery or notebook paper routinely get rejected, usually without being read. Unfair? Maybe. But a fact, nonetheless. You're competing with writers out there who use heavy bond paper, a fresh ribbon or ink cartridge, new (not used) envelopes, and include sufficient postage on both the outside envelope and SASE.

My first reaction as a new writer was "But I can't afford to do that!" You may feel the same. Not being able to afford things was a belief I'd been raised with; it was as much a part of me as my brown eyes. My related beliefs included "I'll never own a new car," "I'll never take a trip to Europe," "I'll never buy clothes unless they're on sale," "I'll never make more money from my writing than just enough to get by." This deeply-ingrained fear of *not being able to afford anything* can keep your writing career stalled.

Challenge Negative Beliefs

In *Don't Worry, Make Money*, Richard Carlson, Ph.D., says we all have beliefs that get in our way—nagging, habitual convictions that we've come to accept as "just the way things are." This definitely included my *"I can't afford that"* litany. "Does this belief help me get things done?" Carlson asks. "Of course not! Does it bring me joy? No. Any effect this belief has is strictly negative."

So change it. Accept the fact that, initially, you will have to spend **some** money to make money, although not nearly as much as you may think. For example, at my early book signings, teachers asked if I gave speeches in schools and if so, how could they contact me? Flustered, I scrambled for a notepad or scrap of paper and scribbled my name and phone number. I didn't hear from many of those teachers.

But after I invested a small sum of money to have professional business cards printed, things changed! When I had a business card to hand out, I often received one in return with the contact's name on it; I heard from one-third to one-half of them later. I couldn't expect teachers to take me seriously if I didn't take my own business seriously. (The money I spent on 500 business cards was more than earned back with the first speech I gave.)

Investing for Your Future

If you have more money and can think in larger terms, consider investing in a computer with plenty of memory. Writing opportunities are growing online, and it's a great way to make contacts and network without ever leaving home. I've only upgraded computers twice, but each time I did it with a specific financial project or purpose in mind—and paid for my investment each time within months. As David Beaird, film director, once said, "Throw your money in the direction you want to go and the rest will follow."

This "spending money to make money" has probably been the hardest money concept for me to wrap my mind around as a writer, but it definitely changed my bottom line from red to black.

---

(3) Think BIG. I tend to think small, not big. But in *Don't Worry, Make Money*, Carlson says, "Thinking big is a magic door opener that broadens your perspective and allows you to see new opportunities." That makes life more fun, and large profits from your writing business a lot more probable.

Many of us think small because we believe it's somehow safer. It's "safe" to submit to small nonpaying magazines instead of the glossy magazine you really want to be published in. It seems safer to approach small presses than large publishing houses. (This in no way diminishes the importance of small presses and magazines—I enjoy them myself. It's a principle I'm talking about here.) If you write the best article you can—with excellent research, tightly crafted prose, an opening with punch, a detailed bibliography—it will take you the same amount of time to produce whether you submit it to a magazine that pays $500 per article or one that pays in free copies. Where is your time best spent? Shouldn't you at least "think big" and try for that glossy, high-paying market?

The primary reason many people think too small is fear. Is your vision too small? Could you be thinking in larger terms? In most cases, the answer is yes! If you agree that your vision as a writer needs to be enlarged, first study your relationship with money. Think bigger, then find a way to financially support that vision until your writing can support you!

Money Maxims

The More Things Change . . .

While the *love* of money may be the root of all evil, the *lack* of money is the root of anxiety in many writers' lives. This situation hasn't changed much over the decades either. Read what other writers down through the ages have had to say about money troubles. On the one hand, you may be aghast at how little progress has been made. On the other hand, today's writers struggling to make money at their craft are in very distinguished company!

"Sir, no man but a blockhead ever wrote except for money." So said Samuel Johnson. I guess I know a lot of blockheads. Most of us would quit if we only wrote for money. Louis Untermeyer expanded on this when he said: **"Write out of love; write out of instinct; write out of reason. But always for money."** The motive for writing is something that every writer wrestles with, especially if the money is a long time in coming. I believe it *will* arrive, in the long run, but it comes to those with persistence and patient endurance. It seldom follows on the heels of our first submissions.

"Write without pay until somebody offers pay," Mark Twain once said. **"If nobody offers within three years, sawing wood is what you were intended for."** Actually, three years is a long time to write without selling something, and I admire writers who stick with writing that long without payment. Each writer must decide for himself how long he can keep writing without some monetary feedback. I might have quit within two years; yet I have friends who persisted for nearly 10 years without selling anything, only to finally sell the first of many fine novels.

"I've never written a book because there's going to be a lot of money in it," says Norman Mailer. **"I know that's the surest way to take five years off your life."** It's an odd paradox in writing, but it can be as true of the rich and famous as the lesser-well-knowns. When we write strictly for the money, the money often eludes us. The "deal" never quite pans out. Or our surefire best-seller falls off the band wagon. Or the book fails to earn back its advance. Conversely, it can be the book that burns within us, that we write with passion and *without* an eye on the dollar sign, that takes off and makes the most money.

"Almost anyone can be an author; the business is to collect money and fame from this state of being." I would say A.A. Milne had a realistic grasp on the publishing business! Even today, almost anyone can call herself an author. All you need is a used computer or typewriter. You can even post your work on your own web pages. Technically, then, you're a "published" author. However, as in A.A. Milne's time, it's still collecting money and fame that's the real challenge!

"The profession of book-writing makes horse racing seem like a solid, stable business," according to John Steinbeck. In many ways, he's right. A newly published book bucks a lot of odds in order to win a race and make some money for the publisher and author. It's decidedly a gamble, full of ups and downs. If you write for a living, you need to factor the "feast or famine" cycle of the writing profession into your plans. You bank your advance for the coming lean months instead of blowing it on a month-long cruise. You write daily, improving your craft, and submit to markets you've carefully studied, thus improving your chances of winning the race to publication. But no matter how much you sell, or how long you write, sometimes a day at the track will look like a sure bet compared to writing!

"Writing is the hardest way of earning a living, with the possible exception of wrestling alligators," said Olin Miller. Anyone who's battled writer's block or bad reviews or lost manuscripts for several months might actually prefer tackling an alligator. At least it'd be a chance to wrestle with something concrete.

"I'd like to have money. And I'd like to be a good writer," said pragmatic Dorothy Parker. **"These two can come together, and I hope they will, but if that's too adorable, I'd rather have money."** On the days the rent is due, I'd rather have the money too. I'd love to write deathless prose, but if that's not possible, I still want to put food on the table. I do, however, firmly believe that you can make money *and* be a good writer at the same time. Whether you're writing the next Newbery book or a recipe for a grade-school magazine, it can *(and should be)* your best possible writing at that time.

"The dubious privilege of a freelance writer is he's given the freedom to starve anywhere," says S.J. Perelman. Well, that's certainly true. Even after being established in the publishing world (as "established" as anyone ever gets), most writers still live from book to book or assignment to assignment. Royalties are iffy, and can't be counted on. And yet . . . when disgusted and discouraged writers decide to return to the 9 to 5 grind so they won't have to worry where their next meal is coming from, it's a decision that usually lasts less than 24 hours. The loss of cherished freedom—even the "freedom to starve"—is too much!

"You must avoid giving hostages to fortune, like getting an expensive wife, an expensive house, and a style of living that never lets you afford the time to take the chance to write what you wish." Such wise words from Irwin Shaw. Watch your style of living. Keep it simple. Drive older cars with low insurance and no payments. Cultivate free entertainment, like museums and hikes and home movies and talking to your family. Pay for things with cash. Haunt garage sales and flea markets. Make do. Wear things out. Dare to be out of step with our materialistic world. That will stretch your writing income dramatically and, like Irwin Shaw, "afford you the chance to write what you wish." ***And, after all, isn't that why we became writers in the first place?***

Stop! Don't Shoot!

Don't be like the legendary gunslinger who marched down the street in spurs that "jingled, jangled, jingled," fixed his beady eye on the villain, and yelled, "Draw!" Why not? Because his shiny six-gun stuck in his holster. When he pulled the trigger, he shot himself in the foot.

What in the world does this gunslinger have to do with you and your writing? Plenty.

Early in our careers (and by early, I mean anytime in the first three years of writing), authors get bitten by a bug. This bug causes a raging fever, accompanied by an agitation with our current lifestyle. We conclude there's only one possible solution to this mental frenzy: **we must quit our day job!**

Ready, Set, Go!

I've been bitten by this particular bug three times in my 20-year writing career. I couldn't stand my day job anymore, and I HAD to have more time for my writing. Deep down I knew I could make a living as a writer. That day job was standing in my way, draining my creative energies. Mistaking frustration for inspiration, I quit my job. **I shot myself in the foot.**

I'm sure you've guessed the ending to this story. The exhilaration of having all day to write evaporated quickly when the bills piled up. During this period I *did* receive more acceptances for my stories—actually many more—but the time that elapsed between writing the story and receiving an acceptance and actually getting *paid* for it created a major cash flow problem. Pressure mounted.

At home I cut expenses to the bone, but it was soon apparent that I had done more than shoot myself in the foot. I had jumped ship without a life jacket. I had not looked before I leaped. I had jumped the gun. (Goodness, why are there so many metaphors for making stupid, impulsive decisions?)

Like Sands through an Hourglass . . .

There's no getting around it. Success takes time. As Jacquelyn Denalli once said, "It takes so doggone long to become self-supporting. That's the one thing that scares a lot of freelancers off; they're good writers and they try it for six months, but when they don't make a lot of money right away, they either give up or are forced to give up because they can't negotiate payment on publication with the electric company."

This happened to a student of mine, a teacher whose husband was in school part-time.

Her family required her income for at least another two years, yet against my advice, she resigned in the middle of the school year. She's an excellent writer, and I'm confident her book will sell, but after a few short months it was apparent she needed her day job to keep food on the table. She ended up delivering pizzas because her teaching position had been filled.

Take Inventory

So . . . before you give up your job to become a self-supporting full-time writer, pause and *honestly* consider these questions.

*(1) **Do you manage time well?*** Is discipline no longer a big problem for you? Writers who have been squeezing in writing hours among regular jobs, household chores, and family obligations often enter full-time life figuring they'll now have all the time in the world. Unfortunately, too much time often leads to procrastination and *less productivity* than a busy part-timer might achieve. So be honest: have you proved to be self-disciplined and motivated in the past? Are you already able to stick to a writing schedule almost every day, no matter what your family or friends are doing? Do you continually start and finish new writing projects?

*(2) **Do you have sufficient financial support to keep you afloat for a minimum of six months, preferably a year or more, if you don't make much money freelancing?*** If you're married, can your spouse carry the whole load that long, and is s/he willing? You really should have six to twelve months' worth of living expenses socked away in savings. ***(This is the most ignored suggestion; it may be the most critical to your success.)***

*(3) **Do you have a business plan?*** Do you have some writing successes already? Know the markets you want to approach, and take the necessary time *beforehand* to study in the specific areas where you want to publish. Do you study current market guides already, and read books/magazines/bulletins in your genre? That's critical. You also need to be keeping careful records of income, expenses, and taxes.

*(4) **Do you have private space for an office where you can work undisturbed when you need to?*** It doesn't have to be fancy (my first office was a tiny closet painted orange), but you'll need good lighting, an answering machine, decent office equipment, and a comfortable chair. You need space of your own [a] to be able to leave your work out (without anyone rearranging your manuscript pages or coloring pictures on them), [b] to work without being disturbed (by the family room TV), and [c] to feel like a professional (which is hard to do when mopping up milk off your manuscript at the kitchen table).

Calculated Risks

I don't mean to imply that you shouldn't try full-time freelancing until you've eliminated every single risk. For one thing, I don't believe you can. There is no such thing as the perfectly safe time to quit your day job, a time where it will be risk-free to be a freelancer. If and when you make the break, it will always require a leap of faith.

However, do strive for balance, for being responsible and sensible, especially if others depend on you. You owe them that. (Obviously, if you're single and without family or financial obligations, making the break will be less of a risk.) Let me repeat: strive for balance. While you owe something to your family, you owe yourself something too.

Slow and Steady Wins the Race

Is all this said to discourage you from ever making the break from your day job to full-time freelancing? *Not at all!* Being a full-time writer is as fun and free and gratifying as you think it will be.

I just want to save you from the agony of leaping too soon, without a safety net, spraining both ankles, then having to crawl back to your employer. So much of our creativity depends on how we feel about ourselves and our writing; being forced to give up puts a real dent in our egos.

Making the change slowly gives you a much higher chance of succeeding. Moving too quickly ("I have to quit *now*!") can actually be your downfall. Having to admit failure can be so discouraging that it is the death of your writing dreams.

Count the Cost

Better, I believe, to count the cost first. See where you are. See where you want to be. Then plot sure and steady steps to reach that full-time freelancing goal. Plan your work, and work your plan.

Then you'll be able to strap on your six-gun, jingle your silver spurs, and (instead of shooting yourself in the foot), take down that villain with a single well-aimed bullet.

Great Expectations

I t's a fact. Some writers start out in more promising circumstances than others. Some have more innate talent, or live in New York with publishing connections, or have hours of spare time every day, or have better training.

Favorable conditions, however, are only one factor in determining financial success for writers. One often overlooked factor is our expectations, according to Paula Ann Monroe in her book *Left-Brain Finance for Right-Brain People.* She claims that low expectations are the villain, the culprit that holds us back financially.

Actions Speak Louder . . .

Low expectations manifest themselves in many ways. They can actually blind us from trying new experiences or seeing publishing opportunities right under our noses. Low expectations can keep us from submitting to publications that pay well, or asking for more money in a contract, or even writing a follow-up letter demanding payment for an article already published! Few of us expect to be paid well for our writing, and such actions reveal this.

Writers' Woes

Low expectations are often caught from other well-meaning writers. We all know the odds against making a living as a writer—or think we do. We all know that plumbers earn a better hourly wage than writers. We all know (and proclaim loudly) that less than 5% of the country's writers can support themselves with their writing. So it's understandable that we start out with, and continue to struggle with, very low financial expectations for ourselves.

Understandable? *Yes.* Necessary or helpful? ***Absolutely not!***

According to Monroe, "Expectations are magnetic. Whether conscious or unconscious, they will rule your behavior. **What you expect, you fulfill.** Therefore, assume you will have wealth (or more wealth), and you will see moneymaking opportunities. What you expect usually happens." If this is true, and if we assume success in publication, will we see more publishing opportunities? If we expect to sell our writing, will we fulfill that expectation? **Pie-in-the-sky as that may sound, that tends to be the case!**

Wealth Consciousness

What exactly do the money experts mean by high financial expectations and successful attitudes? They talk about things like "wealth consciousness," an awareness that there is always plenty of money to go around. Successful people living the abundant life don't worry about having enough—they know that wealth creates more wealth. To a large extent, whether or not you succeed as a writer is a function of your expectations.

> ## Looked in the Mirror Lately?
>
> To succeed financially as a writer, a doggedly positive self-image is as important as publishing goals. Self-concept and attitude play a critical role. The mind needs to accept higher levels of financial prosperity before this can actually happen. In other words, before changes occur in your savings account or publishing record, changes need to occur in your mind and attitudes. You need to weed out those low expectations: "I'll never be able to write for a living," "I'll never publish with a national magazine," "No one will buy this book."
>
> It was said centuries ago that "as a man thinketh in his heart, so is he." It's as true today as when it was recorded. So begin to think of yourself as a writer who will publish, and publish often, who will be respected and read, who will have financial returns for your writing investment. Fully expect your future to turn out this way—and chances are very good that it will.

How Does It Work?

"Oh, come on," you say with curled lip, "will changing my expectations really make any difference?" The money experts seem to think so, as do thousands of writers who have succeeded against all the odds mentioned earlier. We create what we see and what we *expect* to see, either positively or negatively. If we enter into a situation with negative expectations, we will tend to create negative results. Most of us admit that this is true in relationships, or on vacation trips, or even when trying to lose a few pounds. We tend to receive what we believe and expect. Why shouldn't this also be true for a writer entering the publishing world?

Most of us refuse to get our hopes up out of fear. We think we are protecting ourselves. If we have low expectations financially for our writing, then we won't be so disappointed (we hope) when we don't sell much. Is this an effective way to save ourselves grief? Not in my experience. Pessimistic writers with low expectations actually seem to feel *worse* about rejections (not better) than those optimistic writers who aim high. Optimists seem to believe that, because no one *really* knows what's going to happen, it's wiser and more pleasant to assume and expect the best. They bounce back faster from rejection and are much quicker to get that manuscript back in the mail.

Raising Your Expectations and Publishing Success

One of the most basic laws of success is that your energy follows your attention. If your attention or energy or expectations are largely focused on abundance, that is what you will have. You tend to get what you look for, no matter what the area. If you walk down the street expecting people to be friendly, you'll smile more yourself and receive at least 50% more smiles than the gloomy fellow who knows the town is full of old cranks.

The same holds true for writers. Who do you think will write the most enthusiastic, attention-getting query letter? The writer who expects an editor will be as excited by his idea as he is? Or the writer who just *knows* nobody will even read his submission before stuffing it back into his SASE?

Fluctuations and Fortunes

Then consider the ups and downs of the marketplace. Which writer will remain financially stable during these changes? I put my money on the writer with high expectations. He won't be easily discouraged. He will look immediately for other markets that will want his work. When his editor leaves or his publisher folds, he will hunt until he finds another publisher because he fully expects to be successful. A person with a positive outlook views a closed door as an opportunity to strike out in a new direction.

Give It Some Thought

According to Monroe, "We are just beginning to understand that thoughts, although intangible, have tremendous power. **Positive thoughts [expectations] can change perspective, transform behaviors, and attract good fortune.**" Are you a writer who is struggling financially or who wants to make more money from your writing? Then do what the experts advise: give your financial thoughts some thought. Think abundantly!

Bite the Bullet!

In the good old days, newlyweds expected to use hand-me-down furniture, garage sale appliances, and bedroom sets they grew up with. They bought unfinished chairs, glued them together, stained and varnished them, then used them as they saved to buy new things. Today, however, many newlyweds act as if they've been married 25 years already. They buy the best of everything brand new, to which they somehow feel entitled.

This same phenomenon strikes new writers, and it can ruin you financially before you have a chance to get your feet firmly planted.

Reality Check

Too often, beginning writers don't want to act (in a financial way) like beginning writers. They feel that they must have the same equipment established writers own. This can get them in trouble, causing financial pressure that isn't necessary and that strangles the creative spirit.

What does this mean in practical terms? It might mean . . .

(1) You don't put a brand new computer on your MasterCard because your friend has one.
(2) You don't quit your day job to write full-time when you've only sold two short stories in the past year.
(3) You don't sign up for four writers' conferences at $300 apiece when you're having trouble making your car payment.

Delayed Gratification

I'm not sure where the idea originated that beginning writers must start their careers with new computers, color jet printers, Internet access, and attendance at major (expensive) writers' conferences. But I'm seeing it more and more all the time. Unless you are independently wealthy, or are married to someone who is, try to rid your thinking of the idea that you must have all these things *immediately*.

In other words, **it's okay** to start out using your mother's old typewriter.

It's okay to type on the backs of old manuscripts until you type final copy to submit to an editor.

It's okay to read writers' magazines at the library instead of paying for subscriptions.

It's okay to do your research the old-fashioned way, checking out books at the library, instead of surfing the Web.

It's okay to write letters to your writer friends instead of chatting online.

It's okay to read condensed versions and transcripts of writers' conferences rather than attend in person.

It's okay—and very smart—to live within your writer's income until it grows accordingly.

Track Your Expenditures

For the next few months, keep close track of all your writing expenditures. Write down the amounts spent, what goods or services you purchased, and the dates. Scrutinize them. Are any of these expenditures *wants* instead of needs? If they're truly needs, were there other ways of meeting those needs that might have cost less money?

Brainstorm with other writer friends about ways to save money. Make a game out of it. How can you satisfy this need or that want without actually spending money for it? (You'd be amazed how often this is possible if you put your mind to it.) Get into this mental scrutinizing habit each time you want to buy writing-related items.

Do the Math

I don't make as much money from my writing as some people, but my standard of living is quite comfortable. This is due, in large part, to the fact that I keep my expenditures down. It sounds so obvious, but to some it comes as a shock: your spendable income equals what your writing brings in MINUS your expenditures. Sometimes we slave and sweat to increase our writing income, working longer hours and poring over market guides, when we could more easily increase our spendable income by adjusting our expenditures, both one-time purchases and ongoing monthly expenses.

Your Time Will Come

Dorothy Parker once said, "I don't know much about being a millionaire, but I'll bet I'd be darling at it." I bet we all could be!

But until that happens, don't be afraid to bite the bullet when you're getting started. All the fancy extras are nice, but they won't make you a better writer. Only writing—and writing often—will ultimately do that. As one sage said, "If you write poorly now, with a computer you can write poorly faster."

So take it slow. Your income will grow naturally, and someday you'll be able to afford and appreciate the "extras."

Get Your Family Involved

Are you a working writer with children? If so, you'll often be advised to enlist the support of your family. That can be a constant uphill battle unless you do something else as well: get them involved in the writing itself.

Getting Help

What's usually meant by enlisting the support of your family? When my kids were toddlers and preschoolers, enlisting their help meant asking them to play outside quietly while I worked. As they got older, it meant "older" things: cooking simple meals, folding laundry, vacuuming, running errands once they could drive, baby-sitting younger siblings when I had a deadline, screening phone calls.

All of this is fine and good—and necessary. However, unless you want "enlisting support" to be a daily challenge, you need to expand your definition of that support. Try motivating your family by getting them **involved** in what you do.

A Family Priority

If you don't want your writing to threaten your family—and it will threaten many children—ask more of them than just helping with chores. Make their active involvement important to your success. Then they'll want to help you, swimming alongside you instead of swimming against the current and sapping the energy you need for writing.

How do you get your family to feel important to your writing process? In a variety of ways, again depending on their ages.

Real Involvement

Before I was online, I had my middle school daughter do research for me at the library. I would list topics or questions (about sea horses and bonsai trees, for example) and ask her to find books on those subjects. She walked uptown and returned with everything our small library had on the subject. I easily found the information I needed for my story. And my daughter was proud of the help she'd provided, which I, of course, discussed with the family at the supper table. She glowed as I described the work of my "research assistant."

Sometimes the children became photo subjects for various articles, such as how-to, step-by-step pictures for craft articles. When writing fiction, I sometimes had them pose in various settings and outfits when I needed character descriptions. I even used the video camera to record certain actions that I needed to describe in detail in my book (a child climbing a tree for my mystery, one child chasing another, children playing with six-week-old kittens, etc.). Then I'd watch the videos over and over, pausing to make notes. These photos and video clips were shared with the kids' dad and grandparents. I also shared the published story, showing the child where I used that information.

School-age children can help with your promotions: stuffing envelopes when doing mailings to schools or education agencies, sticking printed labels on the envelopes, stamping them.

> Take your family along on research trips whenever possible. I write mysteries set in my home state, so I take pictures on vacations and day trips. The kids pose in the pictures. They also keep their eyes peeled when walking or driving through locations for unusual or interesting objects, people or buildings to photograph. (This does double duty. Besides getting them involved, it also shows me what a child finds interesting. Trust me: your kids will point out people and things down at their eye level that you would walk blindly by.)

Test writing-related projects on your family. When working on a mystery where the mother was a new caterer of ethnic foods, I had to learn to cook them like the mother in the book. My family watched me, then did the taste tests. The kids' reactions were sometimes lifted verbatim for my books.

Children are great for help with names: character names, pet names (which give me particular trouble), group or club names, school project ideas, etc. Again, show the children which names you used in your story, both in the manuscript and when it's published. Even if they can't read yet, point out the words and thank them for their help.

Involve them in all aspects of your writing. When I was packing for the Highlights Chautauqua Workshop, my older kids wanted to help. So I asked them to find me the missing travel iron, my umbrella that had wandered off again, some hot chocolate and hot pot, and many other "comforts from home." They gladly helped me find these things. When I called home during the week, I mentioned how the umbrella had saved my books and hair during a storm, and how unwrinkled I was since my daughter found my travel iron. And I wasn't pretending. I think this is important. I *would* have been drenched and wrinkled without the umbrella and iron; they *did* help me by finding these things.

Team Playing

So don't just enlist your family's support. Get them involved. You're a team. Don't leave them sitting on the bench to watch you play. Ask them to come out on the field and get involved in winning the game. No one likes to be benched—that's where those left-out, unwanted feelings come from. Left untreated, those left-out feelings can grow so much that your family will actually seem to play on the opposite team, trying to defeat you.

Make your writing success a family affair. Encourage the "we're in this together" feeling. If you do, you won't have to wait for anyone to form a fan club for you. You'll have the best one possible, right there in your own home.

8 Strategies for Being Your Own Agent

N ew writers often ask if I have an agent and are surprised to find out that *no*, I don't, and *no*, I never did, and *no*, I don't want one. The second question is always, "Then how do you negotiate your contracts with publishers?" The answer, of course, is the same as how two porcupines make love: very carefully.

Negotiation has two sides, each side wanting to get the best deal possible, but it shouldn't be adversarial. *Both* parties want to come to an agreement, and it is in their best interests to do so. Don't charge in, expecting to get everything you ask for. At the other extreme, don't be too timid or feel as if there is something unseemly about questioning the terms being offered, or asking for more. To be your own agent, take the job seriously and employ the following strategies for success.

Strategies

(1) Educate yourself. If you're going to negotiate your own contracts, you must educate

yourself if you expect to do so in a professional manner. You must understand basic terms and what can be expected for various kinds of contracts. Be ready! After an editor reads your manuscript, the offer to publish may first come by phone; terms discussed involve advance payments, the royalty, and whether the book will be hardcover or paperback (or both). Take notes during this phone call, and ask questions if you don't understand.

The call (if there was one) is followed by a written contract. The money and terms offered are not pulled out of thin air. The offer comes after much figuring in the editorial office, a financial analysis of expected sales and returns, retail price, manufacturing costs, cover art, any illustrations, etc. Educate yourself so that you know what is considered a poor/average/good advance and royalty for the genre and age group you write for. Study books like *How to Understand and Negotiate a Book Contract or Magazine Agreement* by Richard Balkin or *Be Your Own Literary Agent* by Martin P. Levin. Contact organizations like the Authors Guild at www.authorsguild.org, the National Writers Union at www.nwu.org, and the Society of Children's Book Writers and Illustrators at www.scbwi.org.

If you educate yourself on what you can reasonably expect, you'll find it easier to press your position and argue for a better deal than you're offered. Some authors are so happy to be published that they accept offers that are much too low and will hurt future deals. If the editor has come to the point of offering a contract, she really believes in and wants to publish your book. (Please note: I am *not* talking about subsidy or vanity publishers where you pay part or all of the costs of publishing. I am talking about negotiating contracts with commercial publishers who pay YOU for the right to publish your book or magazine piece.)

(2) Prepare. Before you begin negotiating any agreement, go over it with a fine-tooth comb at least two or three times. If you don't understand the terms, look them up in books you own or ask other authors or contact the organizations mentioned above. Make a list of everything you think should be changed. Then decide which things you absolutely must have, which you want but can live without, and which you'd like but don't seriously expect to get. According to Balkin, "Negotiating your own book contract can be like buying a car: You can start the engine and listen, kick the tires, and say, 'I'll take it. How much?' or you can follow the list of directions in *Consumer Reports* and make a thorough inspection of the car, check Edmund's *Used Car Prices*, and then do some hard haggling over the price." It's best to be prepared, so do your homework.

(3) Be quiet and listen. Stay calm, businesslike, and unemotional throughout all negotiations, no matter what your editor says—even if you're offered far worse (or far better!) terms than you expected. Don't interrupt. Take notes while the editor presents her side. She may answer some of your questions if you fully hear her out. According to Gregg Levoy in *This Business of Writing*, "When people are tested for listening skills, they routinely hear between 25 and 50 percent of what was said, and that's under test conditions, immediately after listening to someone." So write things down. If you're talking on the phone, you can't see body language and facial expressions to use as clues, so careful listening is critical. Remember, listening quietly does *not* imply that you agree with everything said. You're just

listening in order to give a careful and appropriate response.

(4) *Confront issues, not people.* Don't be afraid to ask for a better deal. Editors don't withdraw publishing offers because you ask for better terms (unless you're downright abusive or obnoxious about it). The worst-case scenario is that you're told, "Either take my original offer or leave it"—and this doesn't happen often, not with reputable publishers. Be assertive without being aggressive. Lead your editor point by point through the contract, being clear and direct about asking for what you want and need. Keep in mind, though, that there's a big difference between asking and demanding. Be sure you know the difference, watch your tone of voice, and state your position calmly.

Writers are creative handlers of language, so use that to your advantage. Watch how you state things. When discussing what you feel is an unfair clause, there's a world of difference between "I was thinking more in terms of . . ." and "Not on your life, jerk face!" even if your feelings are the same! Your concern is with the *issue* ("payment on publication isn't fair if it's going to be two years away"), not the editor whose job it is to uphold that policy.

Even though this has never happened to me, I know of several cases where negotiations became tense when an otherwise cordial editor turned aggressive and gruff. This is just a tactic. Don't rise to the bait and respond in kind. Keep your mind focused on the points you're making, stay calm, and stick to the issues at hand. When the negotiations are over, this type of editor returns to normal. (Think of lawyers who confront each other in a courtroom, then go out to lunch together when the trial is over.) The editor is confronting the issue, not you.

> **(5) Work for a win-win solution.** Negotiating is not like being at war, with only one side emerging as the winner. Good productive negotiations are conducted so that both sides win, getting as much as they can of what they need. If you're confronted with a contract term that seems wrong or unfair, try to understand what you and your publisher really need, then craft a solution that satisfies you both as nearly as possible.

(6) Ask questions. Much in a publishing contract is negotiable. If something isn't negotiable, your editor will clearly say so. Confirm this with a question like "You mean this can't be changed for any reason under any circumstances?" If the editor says, "That's right," believe it. Then decide if you can accept it. Ask the editor about the purpose of this term or clause. Once each of you understands the other's reasons, it's easier to rewrite the language to suit both parties.

Push for clarity in your contract. Insist that any vague or ambiguous language be changed to language that is clear and unarguable. For example, find out what constitutes an "acceptable manuscript" or "a normal number of free corrections on galley proofs" or what "payment upon signing" means in terms of when you'll actually get your money.

If you're not happy with something as it's written, suggest specific language to replace it. (This is where educating yourself will have paid off.) Feel free to suggest alternatives, offer options, and propose compromises. Offer tradeoffs too. Once I couldn't get my advance increased, so I asked for free books. Instead of the usual ten free hardcover copies, I got two boxes of them, which I promptly sold for full price at school visits, doubling my advance in the process. Be flexible.

(7) Know when to stand fast. Remember the list you made about what points were not negotiable? Keep that list in sight when talking with your editor. Remind yourself that you'd rather pass up the deal than do without the items that were not negotiable. If something is truly unacceptable to you, don't accept it. I know many writers—including myself—who have passed up contracts that weren't fair. I also know many writers—including myself—who signed unfair contracts because they were desperate to publish. Most of us lived to regret doing so as we encountered one problem after another, the least of which was getting paid.

Also remember that rights can be divided and bargained with many times. You can divide by time (electronic rights for six months, after which they revert to the author). You can divide by geography (selling the right to publish in North America, but not elsewhere). Rights are divided by format (hard copy, reprints, electronic, foreign). Be creative when devising compromises, and often you'll find a solution both parties can be happy with.

(8) Get it in writing. Don't assume it's a "done deal" just because you've had an offer over

the phone. After the contract comes and you've negotiated over the phone, take another day or two to decide if you're completely sure about it. Once you've said yes, even if only verbally, that part of the negotiations is closed. If you need more time to consider something, say so, and insist on taking it. No editor will withdraw or worsen a deal because you've asked for a few days to study the matter.

Caution: Remember that your goal in negotiating is twofold. You want to get the best deal you can, but you also want to maintain diplomatic relations with your editor. Be considerate and polite and respectful at all times. Don't be so focused on winning the negotiation battle that you lose the war—and your publisher.

Waiting! Waiting! Waiting!

For a writer, which activity lasts longest?

    A. Submitting a manuscript, proposal, or query.
    B. Waiting for a reply.
    C. Opening your acceptance letter.

Dumb question, right?

Anyone who's been a writer for more than six months knows that the majority of a writer's time—perhaps as much as 80-90%— is spent waiting on the fate of a manuscript or proposal or query. Submitting requires a trip to the post office or sending an e-mail attachment. Accepting requires a trip to your mailbox or e-mail Inbox. It's all that waiting in the middle that separates the men from the boys, the wannabes from the real writers. It stands to reason, then, that if you're going to enjoy the writer's life, you'd better learn how to enjoy waiting.

Enjoy Waiting?

Over and over, seasoned writers tell us that we must learn to enjoy the writing process, the day-to-day putting words on paper that is the essence of a real writer's life. That makes sense, and once we make up our minds to it, learning to enjoy the writing process is a fairly simple matter.

But enjoy the *waiting* process? How? It takes more than just knowing the reasons. Understanding intellectually why we wait so long for a reply (down-sized publishing staff, floods of submissions, holiday vacations) doesn't make waiting any easier.

Ways We Wait

There are at least three different ways we wait, and not all of them are productive.

(1) We wait in a state of high anxiety.

When we're anxious about a manuscript or query that we've submitted, we wait on pins and needles. We know the market guide said "replies within two months," so we give the editor an extra week beyond that. Then our waiting wears thin. Nothing is happening! We decide to help the editor along by taking things into our own hands.

We call the editor. We e-mail the editor. We send an urgent reminder note on neon-pink paper. We aggravate our ulcer and irritate our writing group with our agonizing. Then we have to live with the consequences of what (in haste) we decided to do. In a calmer, dreadful moment, we realize our strident questions angered the editor when we phoned. In retrospect we realize our pink stationery looked amateurish. Our anticipated check is already being spent on antacids, and our writer friends are ignoring our ranting e-mails.

(2) We grit our teeth and hang on.

Others of us wait by clenching our jaws and furrowing our brows. While this is better than making an irate phone call to an editor, it still isn't an enjoyable way to live. For one thing, it tarnishes the daily joy of working on our current writing project. It can also lead to depression, a "what's the use?" feeling about writing. As time goes by, we write less and less. Our enthusiasm wanes.

This is the time when negative things start coming out of our mouths about insensitive editors and the stupid snail mail and what rotten writers we really are. Jealousy of others' success can rear its ugly head now, too. Waiting in this fashion will bring out the worst in you.

(3) We wait with hope.

The writer who accepts that waiting is simply part of the writing game appreciates every small encouragement that comes her way. Perhaps it's a scribbled note from an editor on a rejection slip. Perhaps it's a comment from a critique group member that makes her realize how well she writes from the heart and touches others. Maybe it's just an article in a writers' magazine that, out of the blue, gives her a brand new market to try that looks just perfect!

Even if this writer doesn't publish any more stories or books than the writer who waits with gritted teeth, she'll be a lot more fun to be around! This kind of writer also tends to be more open to constructive criticism, which will provide opportunities for improvement (and thus more sales).

Learn to Wait Well!

As writers, we'll wait no matter what we do. Our attitude and actions during the wait will determine whether we enjoy the trip. In many cases, they'll also determine the length of the wait. Harass an overworked editor, and even if your manuscript was near the top of the pile, don't be surprised if it gets "lost" for a while.

Stay on an even keel. Riding an anxious emotional roller coaster only destroys the time you should be productively writing and studying and improving your craft.

Let someone else attend the pity parties. You stay home and write. Feeling sorry for ourselves will only sap our energy, energy needed for the current manuscript, the one that's even better than the one we submitted months ago. Self-pity leads to jealousy of others' good fortune, and we conveniently forget how long they waited for *their* good news.

Patience Produces Enjoyment

Remember: no one is making us write. We've chosen this business. And just as getting thrown from a bucking bronco comes with the rodeo lifestyle, waiting comes with the writing lifestyle. Any time we're dealing with other people, as when we submit manuscripts and queries to publishers, we multiply the opportunities for delays. Expect them. Even more importantly, plan for them.

Develop patience. Without it, you won't be able to enjoy the writing life you've created. Fully developed patience will help you get where you want to go!

Choosing a Writers' Conference

New writers all dream of attending a big writers' conference someday. Perhaps the celebrated national conference held every summer in Maui. Or the week-long Highlights Foundation Chautauqua writers' workshop in New York. There are also many smaller state and local writers' conferences—too many to choose from sometimes! So how do you find the right one to attend?

Definition

First, what *is* a writers' conference? It's a meeting where writers, editors, agents, and teachers gather to share their expertise and experience with other writers. Beginning writers (those just starting out and those who've been writing for a while with little publishing success) can get a great deal out of these conferences.

They can learn more about the craft of writing through lectures and classes, they can learn from professionals how to handle the many frustrations of being working writers, they can learn about the business side of writing (taxes, legal contracts, etc.), they can make new friends and valuable contacts in the writing field, and they can find potential members for their own writers' groups when they return home.

Locations

How can you locate a conference that's right for you? There are many sources of such information. First, there are writers' magazines like *Writer's Digest* and *The Writer*. They provide annual lists early in the year of the writers' conferences scheduled around the country.

If you're a children's writer, the Society of Children's Book Writers and Illustrators (see their website at www.scbwi.org) is another important source. Once you're a member, you'll get mailings detailing their writing conferences. The bi-monthly newsletter has a section called "Regional News" listing all the children's writing conferences for each state. In addition, there are many online sources for writers' conferences, including: The ShawGuides to Writers Conferences and Workshops at http://writing.shawguides.com/ and a great directory of Writers Conferences and Centers at http://www.awpwriter.org/wcc/index.htm.

Criteria for Choosing

First, seek the type of conference that fits your general requirements. For children's writers, that usually means children's writing conferences, such as those sponsored by SCBWI. Romance writers should check with Romance Writers of America. Science fiction writers, screen writers, mystery writers, and others all have special conferences.

Second, look at the costs. Sit down and figure out what you can afford, including registration fee, travel to the conference, lodging, and meals. Costs can range from $50 for attending a conference at a college campus within easy driving distance to a couple of thousand dollars for a week away, including plane tickets. Scholarships can help offset such major expenditures, but you need to inquire EARLY about them. They may not be advertised, so register promptly and ask if scholarships are available. Volunteering at the conference can sometimes reduce your registration by half or even get you in free. But again, volunteer early.

Third, find out what amount of time is involved. Will you need to take vacation time from work, or is the conference on the weekend?

Fourth, find out what travel is involved. Can you drive and have your car available? Or would that be more trouble than it's worth? Once you're in the conference area, will you need money for cabs or buses to get to your destination?

Fifth, what are the lodging choices? Inexpensive dorm rooms shared with other writers, with one bathroom for four people? A fancy high-rise hotel with cost to match? Can you commute and sleep at home, or stay with a friend in a nearby city? If you're attending a large conference, you'll want to reserve your lodging early.

Sixth, what are the facilities? A classroom, a huge conference hall, a mountain retreat cabin? Will the lodging have a desk for your laptop? If you're physically handicapped, find out about stairs, available elevators, wheelchair accessibility, and the time allowed between workshop classes for getting from place to place. Are there designated nonsmoking rooms? How big are the sessions (intimate groups of ten or halls of hundreds?) Are meals included, and will they accommodate special food needs? Take ALL of these things into account when choosing a conference. Do some digging first!

Preparation

How can you prepare for a conference ahead of time so that you get the most for your money? **First,** read everything you can about the conference and save all the brochures and mailings. Read about the speakers and editors who will be there. If you can, read at least one book by each author who'll be teaching a session you want to attend.

Second, give some thought to your goals and how they can best be met at the conference. Is your goal to make contacts? Then think and plan ahead on how to do that (including printing up business cards). Is your goal to learn more about writing? Then zero in on the classes you know you need, the ones that address your weaknesses.

Third, try to make choices ahead of time rather than taking "pot luck." For example, after I applied to attend the Chautauqua conference, I studied the brochure and bios of everyone who was to be there. I knew that we would be assigned both a Manuscript Critique Person and a Personal Mentor (encourager) to meet with during the week. There were several authors and editors I felt would be just right for me, based on what they'd published. (I was interested in middle-grade mysteries and Christian writing.) So after I sent in my application fee and was accepted, I wrote a letter to the conference chairperson asking for specific people for my mentor and critique person. I gave a list of three for each choice. When I got to the conference, I'd been assigned my #1 choice of mentor and my #2 choice of editor. Both were extremely helpful, and I credit them with the eventual sale of the book I was writing then, which later became a series. Had I just taken pot luck as most people do, I could have ended up with very nice people who published science fiction or were illustrators, fields unrelated to my work.

Fourth, determine which of the conference leaders you'd like to meet during the conference and mark on your schedule where they are likely to be and when. This way you can plan to attend any informal pre-dinner or late night gatherings they will be hosting.

Choosing Sessions

Once you arrive at your conference, how do you choose the sessions you want to attend? You can't sign up for them all! For most conferences, you will find concurrently running sessions, so you'll have to choose which to attend. At the larger conferences, the sessions are offered more than once, but there are still choices to make. Don't choose sessions based on where your friends are going. In fact, if you attend with a friend, try to sign up for different sessions, then pool your notes later. You'll get double for your money that way.

Choose the sessions you know will benefit your writing the most. Before you go, define your writing strengths and weaknesses. If you're presently taking a writing class, ask your instructor for an honest opinion about these—your weaknesses especially. If you belong to a critique group, ask the members.

> For example, if your critique group and/or instructor says your dialogue is weak and unrealistic, look for workshops on dialogue. When the sessions are a choice between "Writing Snappy Dialogue" and "Journaling Your Dreams," sign up for the dialogue session no matter how much you love to journal. If you write beautifully but have no business sense, you should choose sessions dealing with organization and taxes and promotion. Sure, you can sign up for sessions that just look like fun. I always do! But to get your money's worth, be sure you first target the sessions that will address your weaknesses.

Lighten Up!

While you're being businesslike and networking and taking notes, don't forget one more vital thing. Enjoy yourself. Enjoy your writing. Enjoy rubbing shoulders with other authors and with editors. **Have fun!**

Body Maintenance

After months of listening to my Ford Festiva rumble like a semi-truck, I detected an even worse engine noise and finally contacted my mechanic. It turned out that my muffler and tailpipe were completely rusted out, my rear brakes were grinding, and the engine was sick. *Why hadn't I come in sooner?* he demanded.

The reason was obvious to me: the car had continued to run (although sounding terrible) and had stopped on command (even if the brakes screeched and scraped). I had no idea I was missing most of the exhaust system or doing damage to something called brake rotors. Oh, and the noise under the hood? Apparently my engine (which holds only four quarts of oil) was down to half a quart. Oops. To say my mechanic rolled his eyes is an understatement.

High Price of Neglect
As you might suspect, driving hadn't been a pleasant experience for a long time. My daughter cringed in embarrassment when people jerked around to stare as we roared by. We nearly

passed out from carbon monoxide fumes if we idled long at a stop sign. Long car trips were grim endurance tests. But how could I expect to enjoy driving when I didn't take care of my vehicle? Worse, by putting off car maintenance, I did expensive damage to my car.

Body Breakdowns

The same thing applies to our bodies and writing, which I discovered the same eye-opening week. It wasn't just car repairs that had gone untreated. I had been seeing spots before my eyes for six months, my ulcer of five years was decidedly worse, and I endured daily stiff neck headaches from long computer hours. I was certainly *not* writing in flow. With the headaches, neck aches, poor vision, and stomach cramps, even the writing I loved was a drag. And—somewhere underneath—I feared I was doing damage to my health, perhaps permanently.

The point? You need to maintain your car if it's going to run smoothly. Likewise, if you expect to write in flow, enjoy your work, and be productive, you must also do "body maintenance."

Danger! Danger!

If you're like me, taking care of personal routine health and medical checkups is way down on your "to do" list, somewhere below organizing your closets and spice racks. I urge you to move it up higher on the list! If you want to enjoy your writing, make your health a priority.

"But I'm just tired and stressed out," you say. "I don't need a doctor. I need a vacation!"

That may certainly be true. There's a way to tell. If you take some time off work to relax, then return feeling refreshed, you've been suffering from fatigue (which may have many causes, including insufficient exercise and poor eating habits). "True burn-out happens by tapping into and draining off our sustaining life-force energy," says C. Diane Ealy, Ph.D. in *The Woman's Book of Creativity.* **"Once this occurs, we may never be able to repair the damage."** [Please read her last sentence several times.]

Wake Up!

We all know we need to eat right, exercise, get enough sleep, and take our vitamins. (That's like putting gas and oil in our cars—necessary, but just the basics.) But how many of us do serious preventive body maintenance?

- Do you get your yearly physical?
- If you're a woman, are you overdue for a mammogram or Pap test?
- If you're a man, are you overdue for prostate screening?
- When's the last time you had your teeth cleaned or checked out that dull toothache?
- Did you let your cold develop into a sinus infection?
- When were your eyes last checked?
- Are you ignoring chest pain, telling yourself it's just heartburn?
- Do you flex your fingers, hoping it's a touch of arthritis, when you fear carpal tunnel?

If we've been parents, most of us memorized when the "well baby" checkups were due, which immunization shots occurred when, and what changes to expect in our child as months and years passed. Yet how many adults really understand or study the physical changes **we** go through? Do we know **our** changing nutritional needs? Do we understand the value of exercise beyond shedding unwanted pounds? Do we know how many debilitating illnesses can be easily cured (or even prevented), if caught in time?

Help at Your Fingertips!

You don't have time to research all that? Well, the Internet makes it so easy to find this information that there's no excuse for ignorance. Type the words "health," "fitness," "nutrition," and "wellness" into your favorite search engine. You won't believe the wealth of excellent sites available. There are health sites specifically for your age group and sex. Numerous medical sites also discuss symptoms and syndromes, offering practical, useful help you can put into practice immediately.

For example, after curing my ulcer and getting my eyes examined, my biggest problem was the stiff neck and accompanying headaches I got after sitting at the keyboard for hours. My online solution? A health website with "Yoga at Your Desk" mini-moves. (I use the upper body/neck/back ones.) It's the best five-minute break you'll find! Making good use of the resources literally at your fingertips will make you more aware of possible ways to improve your wellness lifestyle.

A Lean, Clean Writing Machine

Are you too jittery to sit still and work? Do you keep jumping up and down? We often attribute this syndrome to heavy issues like fear of writing, the Inner Critic, or driving perfectionism. But it could also be too much caffeine or other stimulants. As author Annie Dillard said, "To crank myself . . . I drank coffee in titrated doses. It was a tricky business, requiring the finely tuned judgment of a skilled anesthesiologist. There was a tiny range within which coffee was effective, short of which it was useless, and beyond which, fatal." (From Susan K. Perry's book *Writing in Flow*.)

Some health-conscious writers take it further than that. "I watch what I put into my body—no alcohol, drugs, caffeine," says Sophy Burnham in *For Writers Only*. "I have become so sensitive to my body's claims that now I actually often eat when hungry (imagine!), stop and lie down when tired. It has taken me years to learn to listen for those two simple demands, knowing that I write better when the machinery's warmed up, oiled, clean."

We *all* write better in that state. So stop right now and take a health inventory. What does your body need? Make a few phone calls, set up necessary appointments, and make your health a priority. **Do it now!**

Create the Writing Life You Love

The Shortest Distance

We all know that the shortest distance between two points is a straight line. So to create the writing life you want, you just need to establish two things: your current location and your destination. Then draw a line between these two points and head straight toward your dream goal. Right?

It's Not So Simple

Wrong. For nearly all writers, the shortest distance to a "dream" writing life is NOT a straight line but one that zigzags and meanders, taking side trips into the jungle and occasionally going in circles. Does it have to be this way? Realistically, it probably does.

Does this mean you have no control over your projected path? Not at all. But it *does* mean you have to know four vital things: where you are right now, where you want to go, the terrain you have to cross, and your daily limitations. Knowledge—especially about yourself—is power. *Write these things down!* Once you have this information, you can draw up a map, grab a machete, and start clearing that career path.

If you're unwilling to do this, you may languish for years in overgrown brush or be stuck somewhere in quicksand. While you blame your writer's block on lack of self-discipline or low self-esteem or laziness, it may be something entirely different. Most often it's disguised fear: of people, money, or time. ("You don't have what it takes," whispers the voice of Wilted Ego. "You're too old already," hints the voice of Procrastinator. "You can't make a living as a writer," warns Stern Parent.) Mapping out your career path can silence these annoying voices and drastically reduce this fear.

To do this, answer *in writing* the following four questions:

Where am I?
Where am I in my *life*? Am I fresh out of high school with no job? Am I a young mother of four-year-old twins? Where am I *financially*? Am I the main breadwinner in my family of five? Am I retired and living on a fixed income? Where am I *physically*? Am I dealing with a chronic illness that keeps me house-bound? Am I a specimen of perfect health who requires only five hours of sleep per night? Where am I *emotionally*? Am I just through a divorce? Did my last child just leave the nest? Am I a contented bachelor with enjoyable hobbies and sports interests? All these real-life circumstances impact our creative trajectories.

Where do I want to go?
Not "Where can I realistically go, based on my lack of connections and mediocre talent?" but "Where do I *really* want to go?" Be as specific as possible, whether yours is a short-term goal

("I want to sign up for that writing course"), a mid-career goal ("I want to sell a science arti-cle to *Highlights for Children*"), or a long-term goal ("I want to make a decent living from writing middle-grade fiction and speaking about writing in schools").

What land will I journey through?
While the shortest distance between two points is a straight line, any explorer will tell you that pursuing a straight line through a rain forest requires different skills and equipment from those required to pursue a straight line over the Alps. So it's important to inspect your proposed route and take into account those special aspects of the terrain ahead of you.

Do you dream of writing historical fiction set during the Civil War? Then your journey may take you through an American history class at the local junior college, treks through used bookstores for primary sources and contemporary accounts, and participation in a Civil War reenactment to get a genuine feel for the era. Or maybe your goal is to write and illus-trate science books for young children. In that case, the terrain ahead could involve making numerous museum visits, interviewing authorities in various fields, and producing a portfolio of art samples.

> Negotiating a career path to the life you want requires strategy, ways to deal with the obstacles in your life that may derail you. You need to accept and plan how to work with your basic temperament and biorhythms. If you're a Type-A list maker, accept and build on that. If you write most easily in the afternoons, don't force yourself to get up at 5 a.m. to write just because your critique group leader does.

What are my obstacles and challenges?

You need to accept your life situation. How many hours do you spend at your day job? If you have children, how old are they? Will you need to learn to write during nap times? While waiting up for them to come in from their dates? How is your health? Can you sit and type for four hours without strain, or does your bad back mean you have to move around a lot? Might a voice-activated recorder turn out to be your favorite writing tool?

How's your financial situation? Must you commute to a daily job, and if so, can you write on the train or bus? Can you work part-time and use your mornings to write? Do you have the means to enroll in week-long workshops at rustic retreats?

You also need to take into account your basic personal needs—how much socializing, recreation, quiet time, and space of your own you require. Do you climb the walls after two hours of solitude and find yourself calling friends or running to the mall? Do you enjoy a quiet walk in the early morning hours, or do you require a hard, fast tennis game to unwind?

Can you write at the kitchen table with children underfoot, or do you prefer to stay up to write after the family has gone to bed? Take time to know yourself. Remember, this is not how you think you should be, but how you truly are at your core.

Reinventing Your Life

There are many paths that could connect where you are right now to where you want to be. But your ideal creative life won't spring full-blown out of thin air. The practical working out of your dreams will occur in the day-to-day choices (often very small choices) you make. You'll need to make compromises, devise strategies to fit your changing circumstances, learn new skills, and (remembering that FEAR stands for *F*alse *E*vidence *A*ppearing *R*eal) take some risks.

We each have only 24 hours in a day. How we spend our time is how we spend our life. Sit down and get serious about how you want to spend *yours*. Take into account everything in your life. Then methodically begin to hack your way through the jungle, one day at a time, until you reach your destination—the writing life of your dreams.

Is Full-Time Freelancing for You?

Y ou stand at the end of the diving board, ready to take the plunge. Poised, arms out at your sides, you bounce slightly on the balls of your feet. You've already tested the water and found it inviting. Yet you hesitate. Should you or shouldn't you?

This is how most writers feel when deciding whether or not to take the plunge into full-time freelancing. Most have tested the freelance waters first, and few take the plunge without some healthy publishing credits under their belt. The smartest writers have also socked away at least 12 months' worth of income for paying the bills. But is that enough? If you have the back-up capital and proven writing talent, is that sufficient to make it as a full-time freelancer?

Not by a long shot.

WQ: Writer's Quotient

To think you can make it as a full-time writer simply because you have the necessary writing talent and skills is a delusion. In order to work from home successfully, you need a whole array of characteristics that have nothing to do with talent. So before you take the freelance plunge, carefully consider the following questions. If you answer "no" to any of them, that doesn't mean you can't be a full-time writer. It merely indicates where your weaknesses may lie. Make overcoming these weaknesses a set of goals for the immediate future.

(1) *Do I persevere or do I give up easily?* Rejection goes with writing as calluses go with digging ditches. What is your response in the face of rejection? Do you quit writing for the day (or week) when a favorite story or proposal comes back with a form slip? Or can you put your disappointment aside while you prepare to send the manuscript out again? Precious days and weeks can be lost if you don't have the ability to handle rejection and keep working.

(2) *What is my attention span?* Without someone looking over your shoulder, do you have Attention Deficit Disorder? Be honest about this. If you can't stay at your desk and work without jumping up every 10 minutes, freelancing at home may not work for you. Can you focus for long periods of time? If not, are you willing to learn how? (I had to use a kitchen timer and set it for 15 minutes at a time to keep myself in my chair working.)

(3) *Do I have clear goals, both short- and long-term?* If you aim at nothing, you'll hit your target every time. Staying busy at home all day won't do any good if you don't know where you're headed and can't stay on track. Out in the work world, your boss set your daily and weekly and monthly goals. As a full-time freelancer, you must develop this skill yourself.

If you're deficient in this area, numerous books and websites are available to help you.

---

(4) Can I work without supervision? One way to answer this question is to watch yourself in the office when your boss is away at meetings all day. Do you find yourself hanging out at the water cooler long after your break is officially over? Do you get as much work done as on the days your boss is breathing down your neck? If you can't work without supervision, you'll never survive at home where the TV, phone, friends, and fridge all beckon with daily lures.

---

(5) *Does my work get done on time?* Are your projects finished on time, or (preferably) even a bit early? Do you build in time for interruptions so that you still finish? If you can't meet deadlines, you'll have trouble with editors and publishers. Practice setting writing deadlines with yourself, including interim deadlines for outlining, finishing a rough draft, revising, and submitting the finished product.

(6) *Do I manage my time well?* When your "to do" list is too long to finish, can you choose which tasks are most important and assign priority to them? Or do you "major on the minors" while leaving significant chores unfinished at the end of the day? Can you tell, in the long run, which tasks will impact your job most and which can be put off (or left undone altogether)? When you work at home, the jobs list can be endless, as there's never enough time to read, keep up with markets, and hunt for freelance opportunities. You must know how to prioritize.

(7) *Do I have the proper equipment?* While it's not necessary to have a computer, laser printer, Internet access, and an answering machine if you're just writing part-time, you'll want these minimum tools of the trade if you expect to compete as a full-time writer supporting yourself and/or your family. To compete with other writers, you need to be able to submit manuscripts on disk when asked, or send them as e-mail attachments. As more and more business is being conducted through e-mail and personal websites, you need online access. Are you knowledgeable about search engines and software? If you don't have the proper equipment, can you afford to buy or lease it?

(8) *Do I have a room of my own in which to set up an office?* While working on a corner of the dining room table is fine for a part-time writer, someone who expects to write full-time needs adequate space for computers, printers, file cabinets, supplies, and (preferably) a door that closes for noise and crowd control. It doesn't have to be a big room—as I've said, I worked out of a walk-in closet for years. But if possible, a full-time writer needs a room that's used for full-time writing alone, where you can escape to work no matter what else is going on in the household.

(9) *Is my spouse or partner supportive of my choice to work at home full-time?* To a spouse who still commutes to work, it may appear that you're "just staying home" and not really working. (The myth continues to plague us that writers don't really work. They just type occasionally.) Try hard to work through these issues with family members before you quit your day job. It can be very difficult to write while dealing with active disapproval on the part of those closest to you.

(10) What if I have young children? Are you very flexible, able to handle numerous interruptions without losing your train of thought? I know many, many parents who write with babies and toddlers underfoot. I did it for years myself. If you can't, how are you going to handle child care? Can you afford a babysitter two days a week, or can you trade babysitting with another stay-at-home worker?

Do Your Homework!

Be honest, and take note of the questions to which you had to answer "no." These potential problem areas need to be dealt with *before* you dive into full-time freelancing if you're to stay afloat. But if you have the capital and skills—and if you've *seriously* addressed the issues above—then take the plunge! Come on in. The water's fine!

Success: Horse before the Cart

"What kind of success are you having with your writing?" a good friend asked me recently. I answered her in terms of book contracts signed and columns written, but her question plagued me the whole long drive home. Why? Because I realized I had given the expected answer and an honest answer, but not a *true* answer.

Money and sales no longer defined success for me. Yes, in the eyes of the world, I was a successful writer. The world equates writing success with money and sales and giving speeches. In the beginning I, too, measured success by how many sales I made, the prestige of the magazines I was published in, the size of the publishing house. But truly, the success I currently experienced had nothing to do with money or contracts.

Marching to Whose Drummer?

I found that after winning the struggle to succeed as a writer (according to the accepted definition of success), I still wasn't enjoying it. This was disappointing—and scary. The years of surviving rejections and learning public speaking and seeing a couple of dozen books published should have made me feel satisfied and proud, but it didn't. Why? I had let others define "success" for me—I never even questioned their terms—but it wasn't *my* definition of success.

If you're just starting out on your writing career, let me suggest that you not do what I did. Don't let others define success for you. Otherwise, even when you attain it, you won't truly enjoy it. You can't be "successful" as a writer until you decide FOR YOURSELF what success means to you.

$$$$$$?

Is your writing success defined by money? If so, how much? A high dollar figure? Or just enough so you can quit your day job and play golf twice a week or join a rowing club . . . or simply stay home with your children? (The latter was my motive.) Does writing success equate with a vacation trip each summer? A new computer or DVD player? Or just enough to take the whole crew to McDonald's once a week? You decide. I'm like Pablo Picasso, who said, "I'd like to live like a poor man with lots of money." I like a very simplified life—but with enough money in the bank not to worry!

Prestige?

To you, is writing success the achievement of your first sale, whether or not it's for a paying market? Is it the ego boost of seeing your byline in a magazine or on a book? Is it the honor of being known in your community as a published writer? Success to me, years ago, was attaining the status of being listed in my hometown library's card catalogue!

Freedom?

Does writing success mean choices to you? Is it the flexibility to set your own schedule, whether a 9-to-5 stint or working in the middle of the night when you feel like it? Is it freedom of place—writing at a coffee house or on a park bench? Is it knowing you can find time to attend your son's soccer game after school or to plant and tend an ambitious vegetable garden?

Passion?

If you've had dead-end jobs that were dissatisfying or boring, writing success to you may be doing work you enjoy and feel passion for. It may be writing fiction or nonfiction that moves you or excites you or is helpful to someone else. Perhaps success is using your writing talents for a worthy cause in some voluntary capacity, whether writing for your church newsletter or to further the election of a political candidate you admire.

Career?

Is your writing goal to build a career and support yourself and your family? Then success to you may be finally getting a "go ahead" on your query. It may be acceptance into a class or a workshop or a critique group. Your feelings of success will be influenced by the numbers of sales vs. rejections. You may feel successful when you set up your office, buy business cards and stationery, and finally need a tax accountant.

Very Personally Yours

I defined writing success in many of these ways over the years . . . and that's the thing about success. Your definition may change and evolve; so do a periodic checkup if you had that successful feeling at one time, but seem to have lost it. For me today, success means enjoying the daily process. Was the writing fun today? Was I challenged to learn something new? Did I capture even one new creative thought? Did I "lose" myself in the flow of the writing? If the answer is yes, then it was a very successful day.

Cart before Horse

Too often writers charge full-steam ahead in pursuit of writing success. We take writing courses, buy expensive hardware and software, track down market news and attend writers' conferences—all without deciding what success (to us) even looks like! It's disappointing to reach a goal, only to find it wasn't YOUR goal, but someone else's. So tackle first things first. Decide which qualities define writing success for *you*. Let your horse *pull* the cart instead, and you'll arrive at your writing goals much faster!

Who's in Charge?

"Your life is the sum result of all the choices you make, both consciously and unconsciously," said Robert F. Bennett, U.S. Senator from Utah. "If you can control the process of choosing, you can take control of all aspects of your life. You can find the freedom that comes from being in charge of yourself." I agree. By the same token, your *writing* life is also the sum result of all the choices you make.

Choosing is making a decision each time you come to a particular crossroad. Many decisions are not deliberate. Instead we unconsciously follow our habits, choosing what is easiest because it's what we've done for years. Unfortunately, we may choose negative thoughts about our abilities; we may choose negative attitudes about our progress; and we may follow with negative actions of *not* setting goals and *not* writing.

Choice or Habit?

Although your choices may have become automatic habits, each is still a decision you made. You need to begin noticing your choices, moment by moment. Think about what you're thinking about! Then start making consistently better daily choices. Take control of your writing life by being in charge of yourself.

Writers make critical decisions in three areas every day—sometimes every hour. **Wake up!** Train yourself to be a close observer of your choices. Beginning today, consciously choose the direction that leads to your writing goals.

(1) Thoughts

If you want to make positive changes that last, you may need to change the way you think. Certain thoughts and beliefs can derail you before you even get started. ("I'm not good enough." "I don't have the talent I need." "It's who you know in this business, and I don't know anyone important." "I don't have the time/energy/family support to write.") Take time to recognize which particular issues negatively affect your choice to write.

Perhaps your thoughts about writing contain a few myths that need exploring—and debunking. Do you think you'll be a happy writer if you just manage to get published? You might be—but probably only if you're happy *before* you get published. Grumpy, negative, passive writers who achieve publication tend to be grumpy, negative, passive writers with a publishing credit. Publication itself won't make you happy.

Do you think there's a magical shortcut to writing success? Are you constantly on the lookout for the latest quick-fix writing book or article, the latest get-published-now scheme?

Do you think if you can just find the key, you'll produce a national best-seller? If so, bear in mind that even in this instant-gratification society, excellent writers don't spring up overnight—they are grown. *Slowly.*

Do you think it's someone else's fault that you aren't published? Do you have a general mental habit of blaming your lack of success on others? While it's a human tendency to do so, this kind of thinking will keep you stuck—and unpublished. Every career presents obstacles that must be conquered on the way to success, and writing is no different. The obstacles only change from time to time. (Obviously, writers 50 years ago didn't have to worry about their hard drives crashing!) Writers in all eras have had barriers to overcome. At one time women writers had to disguise what they were doing—and even use male pen names in order to get published!

Choosing your thoughts means noticing when a negative thought passes through your head ("When am I going to get published? I've been submitting for months and months! I should just quit!") and replacing it with "Getting published takes time for all new writers, and if I'm persistent and consistent in my efforts to improve and market well, I *will* get published eventually!" At first, it's reinforcing to say these new thoughts out loud.

(2) Attitudes
Changing your thoughts will change your attitudes and feelings about writing. Instead of postponing happiness until you get published, choose to be content with your writing *today*. Choose

to enjoy the act of putting words down on paper to capture an image. Choose to enjoy delving into your memories for the kernel of a story idea. Choose to enjoy learning about a new subject and tracking down research facts about it. Choose to enjoy the process of reading back issues of magazines you want to submit to. Choose to enjoy revising and polishing your paragraphs.

Instead of feeling pressured to succeed quickly, choose to be patient with your learning curve. Choose to be happy about each small, steady step forward. Look at the large picture, how each writing day is another small building block laying the foundation of your career. Pace yourself with the determined attitude of the tortoise instead of the sprinter attitude of the hare.

> You also need to choose commitment—to your goals and deadlines, to continued improvement in your writing. Commitment is more than "I wish" or "I'd like." Commitment is "I will." There is a huge difference! Move from the wishy-washy attitude of "I'd like to be a writer" to the commitment level of "I'll do whatever it takes for as long as it takes to be a successful writer." Attitudes of self-control and self-discipline will make those small daily changes that add up.

(3) Actions

That committed attitude will make choosing your actions easier. When you're willing to do whatever it takes to revamp your personal life so you can write, the choices become clear. You will do things like choosing to write before doing the dishes, even though it bugs you to leave dirty dishes in the sink. You will choose to write for an hour instead of watching TV or talking on the phone. You will choose to have that lower carb/higher protein lunch so your writing energy is high all afternoon. You will choose to retire at a decent hour so you're alert to create the next morning. You'll consciously make quality time with your family so you can write without feeling guilty.

Instead of settling for a vague mental wish list, you'll choose to set specific goals, write them down, and even put them on a poster on your office wall so you're staring at them daily. You'll choose to settle quarrels and resolve conflicts partly because not doing so saps your writing energy. In all areas of your life, you'll make choices that will support your writing instead of making it more difficult.

Each time you come to a fork in the road, **make a choice and be in charge of your writing.** Each choice may be small, but these decisions add up to your life. Find the freedom that comes from being in charge of yourself—and thus your writing.

No Quick Fixes

We live in an instant society. Computers yield up information in a flash via e-mail and the Internet. Photos are scanned and mailed with the click of a mouse. Fax machines deliver contracts. We guzzle instant coffee, whip through fast food drive-throughs, scoot with our milk and bread through the express check-out lane, grab instant money at the ATM—and if all this hurrying disagrees with us, gobble an antacid for instant relief. It's no wonder we're conditioned to fast, **faster, *fastest*.** And no wonder that many of today's writers are afflicted with an "I-have-to-publish-in-a-hurry" syndrome.

Writers have always *desired* quick publication. Until recently, though, this was rarely possible. After some thrashing about, submitting hurriedly written manuscripts and receiving rejection slips by return mail, we settled down. We accepted the fact that it was going to be a long haul. If we wanted to get published—and for most of us that meant acceptance by national magazines and book publishers—there was no quick fix. There was no instant publishing gratification.

My, How We've Changed!

Not so today. Personal web pages, self-published e-books, and freely posted articles abound on the Internet. You can be "published" within minutes of completing a piece of writing. I wince when I read some of the bad writing that proliferates online today. I'm so glad there was no Internet when I started writing. Being an impatient soul myself, I would have been one of the first to self-publish. I shudder at the idea of my early rejected stories floating in cyberspace. They seemed like deathless prose at the time. But oh, the embarrassment of having anyone see them today!

Why Wait to Publish?

If you're a new writer, you may legitimately ask, "Why wait?" Why not reach for the quick fix of instant publishing gratification? There's really only one reason: you need to take the time to develop your craft, to hone your skills, to go deep inside yourself to find your own themes, your own gut-level stories to tell. *This can't be done quickly.* Unfortunately, many writers today want to point remote controls at their computers and fast-forward through all the "hard, boring stuff."

But when we do that—when we take the shortcuts—we end up with less than our best. We mass produce mediocre work, not the splendid writing we could create if we completed our apprenticeship. And if we want to do splendid work, writing that touches other souls, we need to endure tough times. It's like a boy who desperately wants to be six feet tall: during his growth spurts, he lies awake nights with growing pains in his legs. It hurts to grow sometimes, literally, in our bodies, and figuratively, in our writing. We want to bypass the misery and still reach six feet. We want to publish that award-winner or sell that series—but we'd like to do it without experiencing the pain of rejections, repeated revisions, poor reviews, and thin sales that precede 95% of such "overnight" successes.

"There is more to life than increasing its speed," said Gandhi. Similarly, there is more to the writing life than publishing faster. Deliberately take the time to grow as a writer, to embrace the hard times, the "growing pains" of finding out what you really have to offer the world.

While We Wait

There are many things you can do during this growth period to help further your writing. Study. Write daily. Journal. Observe your world. Broaden your experiences. Acquaint yourself with the markets.

Mostly, though, accept the fact that there are no shortcuts. Accept it at core level. Look at the good things that can come with taking it slow. Settle down inwardly and get ready to grow, as a person, as a writer. Give up the pressure of an inner timetable. Set goals, yes. But set goals *you* can control, like "I will read one book on the craft of writing each month" or "I will send for writers' guidelines for six magazines per week" or "I will write one hour every single day." Setting goals this way, if you're consistent, will take you slowly and steadily toward your success as a writer.

> ## Pull Over!
>
> Mentally picture yourself leaving the express lane at the grocery store and moving to the longest check-out line. Stand still, then move forward slowly. Observe people. Take notes. Think. Slow down both your body and your mind. Enjoy the wait—make that your goal. Breathe deeply. Stop fuming. Stop watching to see how fast the other lines are moving forward. Enjoy where you are. Deliberately take your time.
>
> Go down deeper rather than rushing forward faster. Paradoxically, you'll arrive at your destination—being a successfully published writer—much faster. Take time to build a solid base, a firm foundation, for your career. Then, when the inevitable ups and downs of the publishing world buffet you, you'll stand strong and immovable. You'll go with the publishing flow, writing steadily, accommodating changes in the industry.

The Eventual Reward

As a writer, you have another very good reason for taking things slowly. Creativity cannot be summoned like a genie rubbing a bottle. There is no such thing as instant creativity. "Creativity flourishes not in certainty but in questions," says Sue Monk Kidd, and adds, "Yet the seduction is always security rather than venturing, *instant knowing* rather than deliberate waiting." If you'll take your time and wait deliberately, your creativity will flourish. Good things **DO** come to those (including writers) who wait!

Voices of Self-Sabotage

You've often heard the phrase "you are your own worst enemy." Does this apply to you when trying to create a writing life you love? It certainly applies to me!

How does this enemy within keep you from moving ahead with your writing dreams? By telling you lies. Some are bold-faced lies. Some are wrapped in soft wool. Some lies ridicule you, while others sound downright comforting. What do all these voices in your head have in common?

They're instruments of self-sabotage. They convince you to give up.

Who's Talking Now?

There are many voices inside your head. You must listen and decide who's doing the talking at any particular moment. Some voices are easy to recognize; some are so subtle you'll be shocked.

First, you have the **voice of the Inner Critic**. It whispers words like "What makes you think you have anything interesting to say?" "You're no good." "That junk will never sell." "You're actually going to show that story to somebody?" The Inner Critic beats you down with criticism. Sometimes this voice bears a remarkable similarity to that of your mother, your spouse, or your junior high English teacher.

As Julia Cameron says in *The Artist's Way at Work*, creativity requires a sense of inner safety, something like a fortress. "In order to have one, you must disarm the snipers, traitors, and enemies that may have infiltrated your psyche."

I spent years fighting my Inner Critic's voice with positive affirmations and gritted teeth. "Oh, yes, I can!" was my motto. In time, my Inner Critic was quieted, only speaking out when I got an unexpected rejection or bad review. Yet I still wasn't creating the writing life I dreamed of. Something was holding me back. It took me a long time to realize I still had voices in my head, because the tone and words had changed.

Do any of the following voices live inside your head and keep you from fully pursuing your writing dreams? Listen and see.

Voice of Responsibility

This voice sounds so adult, so sensible. It tells you to grow up, to get your head out of the clouds and your feet back on the ground. "You're neglecting your children (or your job)," says this voice. "Look at your messy kitchen (or yard or garage)." "You have no business hiring someone else to mow the lawn so you can write!" "You'd better walk the poor dog first." Guilt is piled on by this voice, and you crumble under its weight. You put your writing dream on the back burner until a time when you're less burdened by responsibility.

Voice of Intimidation

This voice is snide and cryptic. It slaps your hand when you try to crawl out of the box that is your life and declare yourself a writer. "Who do you think you are?" this voice asks. "You'll make a fool of yourself!"

Doubt and low self-worth take these statements as the truth, and that of course only serves to further lower your self-esteem. Cowering, you crawl back in the box and close the lid on your dreams.

Voice of Fear

We all know this voice; it's been with us since birth. We fear different things, of course, when we declare ourselves as writers. We fear rejection, we fear ridicule, we fear what our loved ones will do. "You're risking your close relationships (with your spouse, parents, children, friends) by committing to your writing," this voice warns. "Why lay yourself and your ego on the line just to get rejected?"

Voice of Compassion

This soothing voice sounds like your best friend or older brother. This voice understands you. It puts an arm around your shoulders and gives you a sympathetic squeeze. "You work so hard; why don't you take a nap or watch that football game on TV instead of writing?" the voice croons. "You've taken on so much, and I worry about you." You certainly agree with this voice. You're exhausted from all the demands already on your life, and you need to take care of yourself. "You'll be a better writer after you're rested and relaxed," this voice assures you as you switch off your computer and head for the couch.

Voice of Procrastination

This voice is a close relative of the voice of compassion, and just as alluring. This voice is a comfort because it reminds you that there's no rush. There's all the time in the world to write that play or story or book proposal. This voice is too smart to tell you to give up on your writing dreams. Instead this reassuring voice says, "You don't have to write that article today. You'll have plenty of time tomorrow."

Be Alert!

Most of what stands between us and writing success is what occurs *inside* us—not in our surrounding environment. So learn to listen to the voices in your inner environment. Argue with the negative ones. Then argue with the comforting ones, if the effect of their advice will be to derail you from your writing dreams. **Be alert.** And learn to be your own best friend instead.

The Traveling Writer

When my last child left the nest for college, my work settled into a reasonably predictable schedule with few interruptions. After 20 years of writing with children and their friends underfoot, it was heavenly.

Then, suddenly, my calendar filled up again. I found my schedule for the coming months included attending a family wedding out of state, helping my daughter when her first baby was born, visiting a friend for a week, and speaking at a conference, also out of state. Each event would mean being gone for an extended period of time. Yet self-employed writers seldom have the luxury of leaving their work behind. They don't get paid vacations, so long breaks add up to time off without pay. Also, if you're in the middle of a writing project (especially fiction), taking substantial time away from work can be disruptive to the flow of the story.

Planning and Flexibility

The alternative was to take my work along on my travels. I knew this would require flexibility and the ability to seize odd moments to write in a variety of circumstances. In the past, I'd grabbed my notebooks or laptop computer and hit the road, only to return a week later with no writing done. This time I decided to think things through and plan ahead. Could I combine my writing and my trips effectively in order to enjoy *both* and not shortchange myself?

Yes! Traveling and writing CAN be combined. With a little forethought, you can manage the necessary tools, times, and places to write.

Tools for the Traveling Writer

If you don't plan ahead, you're likely to find yourself in a motel or on a bus, ready to write but without the tools you need. So pack carefully. Are you taking a laptop computer with you? Then you'll need a charged-up battery or two, any disks or CDs required for the project, a power source, and perhaps an away telephone number for your ISP Internet connection.

If you're keeping a journal on your trip, be sure you have it packed. You may need a smaller notebook that fits in your purse or backpack. What about extra pens and paper? If you do your writing on legal pads, a stiff plastic cover keeps the paper clean and gives you a firm surface on which to write.

Times for the Traveling Writer

When you first peruse your travel schedule, you may feel convinced that there simply won't be any time available for your writing. You may have activities planned (or planned for you) that don't seem to show any gaps of free time. If so, look again.

What about when you check into your motel? Avoid turning on the TV for "company" or to check the local news and weather. Instead, unpack your writing supplies, clean the flyers and TV program listings off the desk, and set up an instant office. If you're staying at someone's house, make up your mind to write while others watch TV or snooze after a big family dinner.

> You can easily find time to write on planes. Just skip watching the movie, ignore the head phones, and leave the in-flight magazines unread. Instead, write longhand or on a laptop on your drop-down table. You can also find time to write on buses and in taxis during long shuttle trips to and from airports. Time spent waiting in airports provides other opportunities to work, whether "people-watching" and jotting notes for your character files or writing longhand while perched on your pile of luggage.

Places for the Traveling Writer

Workplaces for the traveling writer are easy to find. Depending on the nature of your trip, you may find yourself writing on a park bench, at a backyard picnic table at a relative's home, or on the dock of a lakeside resort. If your group is staying in a motel, you can write at a table by the pool or sneak down to the lobby and find a comfortable chair for half an hour. You can write in public libraries. While others in your party shop at the mall, you can write in bookstores that provide chairs and tables. If you've planned a day at the beach, try writing while you tan instead of reading or listening to music.

Other places to write on the road include diners, lunch counters, delis, and coffee shops. And don't forget your bed! Pile up pillows behind your back and grab your notebook or laptop. You can write first thing in the morning if you're a guest in someone's home—just let them think you're sleeping late. Or write in bed before you go to sleep.

Seize the Moment

If your upcoming schedule includes traveling, yet you need or want to keep writing while on the road, do some preplanning before leaving home. Adjust your mind-set ahead of time as well. Be alert to unexpected chances for impromptu writing sessions. Keep your writing tools handy in order to take advantage of these opportunities to write during your day. Be determined to write in whatever chunks of time you find. If you want to travel, but you also need to work, this is one way to have your cake and eat it too!

A Call to Excellence

Have you lost your passion for writing? Is it harder to get to work than it used to be? Is it writer's block or burnout? Not necessarily. You may have lost your passion for writing because you've lost your passion for excellence.

In the beginning of my writing career, even though I was tripping over babies and toddlers, I *made* time to write. I really *studied* magazines and market guides. I bought and read and marked up and re-read many writing craft books. I kept a writer's notebook handy to jot down detailed character and setting descriptions. I did many writing exercises simply to improve my writing—not with an eye toward selling it. I revised and revised and *revised*. I let things "sit" before doing a final editing. I read award-winning books, trying to absorb by osmosis how these writers created imaginary worlds.

I wasn't satisfied to be a good writer—not even a published writer. I wanted to be— tried hard to be—an *excellent* writer. I was rewarded, I think, when my earliest books won awards, landed on many children's choice lists, and went into paperback and foreign editions.

I have never done more satisfying writing in my life.

So What Happened?

But when we turn professional (*i.e.*, begin selling), the emphasis often shifts from sharing our stories and passions with the world to selling the next manuscript, or writing faster, or finding a better agent.

Unfortunately, this shift often changes our priorities. Instead of telling a story with excellence, instead of writing an article based on in-depth research, we may subtly ease up on ourselves. Perhaps we don't do quite as much research. (After all, we only use about 30% of what we unearth anyway.) We write briefer character sketches because (a) they're too time-consuming, (b) we need to get to the *real* writing, and (c) less than half the details in those profiles make it into the finished manuscript.

Speed becomes an issue. We read books on writing faster, making more money per hour, finding hot topics. We don't take time to revise and get critiques and revise some more. Sometimes we can't, if we've become over-committed. With a raft of projects and deadlines, you may still do acceptable work. But will it be your very best work? Nope. The "hurry hurry" shows, and you end up with books you're not proud of, that get poor reviews, and that undermine your writer's self-esteem. "Have I lost it?" you wonder in private. No, you haven't. But when you rush, the writing suffers. It can't help it. And your desire to write diminishes.

Deeper Solutions

What can you do about this spiral? Can you get back the passion for your writing that comes from a commitment to excellence? Yes, I believe you can, but it may require overhauling your entire life. Having an excellent writing life is part of leading a life of excellence—**period**. Writing is only *one part* of your life.

As I remembered the early years of my writing, I realized that not only had I pursued my writing with passion, I had (in spite of many struggles) pursued excellence throughout my life. My four kids were read to, played with, well taken care of. My house was clean, I cooked nutritious meals from scratch, kept a tidy (huge) vegetable garden, and taught classes at church. I even quilted and created homemade Christmas presents.

Now I took a hard look at myself. Boy, had I slipped! As a single empty nester, I ate poorly (lots of fast food), my house was dusty and cluttered, my small flower garden had more weeds than flowers, and I hadn't quilted in 10 years. I wasn't pursuing excellence in any area of my life really. Acceptance of mediocrity—and the dissatisfaction that accompanies it—had settled in.

Back in the Saddle Again . . .

I decided to clean up my life that week. I cooked nutritious meals and froze a week's worth for convenience. I scoured the house and weeded the flower beds. I sorted, filed, then dumped my piles of "stuff."

And there was an odd side benefit. When it was time to write, I found my standards had gone up. I took more pains with my writing: doing the daily exercises, keeping a notebook again, nurturing the muse, ignoring hot topics and returning to my own ideas and passions. As I put more effort into my work, I enjoyed it more. As I enjoyed it more, I worked even harder. Momentum built as I grew excited about my writing again. I relearned an old truth: being stretched and challenged renews our passion for our writing.

Living—and Writing—at a Higher Level

A "call to excellence" will look different for each of us. Strive to live an excellent life, not just one where you get by. If you have a day job, arrive on time, work hard, and take care of your personal business elsewhere. Pay your bills on time. Lose that 20 pounds you gained when you had your last baby (who's now in junior high) or when you stopped playing touch football with the guys on weekends. Cut down on your TV time; watch programs that nourish your mind and spirit. Get exercise and fresh air. Keep commitments and promises, even when you regret agreeing to them.

Believe it or not, deciding to live an excellent *life* will translate into living an excellent *writer's life* too. You—and your readers—deserve that. Don't settle for less.

Taking Time Off

For the first time in 15 years, I took a week off at Thanksgiving. It was my first year as an empty nester, and I let the writing go while I enjoyed my college kids home on break. I dreaded the following Monday morning, though, figuring it would be like pulling teeth to get back to work. I'd always had enough trouble getting started when I wrote every day. Imagine how hard it would be after a week off!

I gritted my teeth, booted up the cold computer, flexed my fingers, and . . . started typing! The first hour flew by, then the second. I was astounded at how much more focused I was. I'd had trouble concentrating for months. Even more exciting to me, my morning's writing was actually fun!

A Contradiction?

Most of us know from sad experience that extended periods of overwork produce burnout. We burn out as writers, we burn out as parents, we burn out on the job. But driven by the "you must write every day!" command, we're afraid to take time off from the writing. We might "lose it." But listen to the English writer Samuel Butler: "To do great work a man must be very idle as well as very industrious." Is this a contradiction? Not really. But there are definite do's and don'ts about how you spend that idle time. To benefit most from taking time off from your writing, try to do the following things.

Time Off Activities

(1) In *Write Where You Live*, Elaine Fantle Shimberg says, "I grew up in Iowa, where farmers rotated crops so they wouldn't wear out the soil. Some years they planted nothing in a particular field and just let it lie fallow, giving it time to re-nourish itself. I think our creative resources need that time to rejuvenate as well."

During down time away from your writing, find a quiet spot and reflect. Think about your past writing successes and the direction your career is headed (or isn't!). Review goals that may have gone by the wayside. Reflection is one great use of time off from your work. Haste makes waste, while several hours spent pondering can save you weeks and months of mistakes that will need correcting later.

(2) As tempting as it is, avoid using time off from your work to overwork in other areas. Instead of making a month's worth of casseroles for the deep freeze, order in a pizza. Instead of washing the car yourself, take it to the car-wash. This is idle time, remember, not a time for cleaning out gutters or rearranging closets. Even "fun" can be overdone to the point of exhaus-

tion. Instead of three days of wilderness backpacking, try a one-day hike and picnic in a state park. Be sure that during your time off you get sufficient rest. Also, eat well. Stick to three balanced meals a day, no matter how tempting it is to eat ice cream for breakfast or a triple order of french fries for dinner. You want to return to your desk healthy and rested, not sick.

---

(3) In *The Artist's Way*, Julia Cameron recommends weekly "artist's dates" as a way to restock the pond of images and experiences we use in our writing. Without sufficient time off, writers are fishing from empty ponds. An artist's date is a block of time set aside—an appointment you make with yourself—when you nurture your inner creative child. It's like a field trip or a play date with yourself. Plan it, and refuse to take anyone along. Anything that nurtures your writing soul can be such a date: a long walk, watching an old movie, going to a concert or museum or second-hand store, an art gallery, the beach, bowling . . . anything you find nurturing.

Benefits of Time Off

Returning to your work after several days or a week off can produce surprising benefits, *if* your time off was spent in some of the productive ways mentioned above. You may find, as I did, that you're able to get into the flow of writing much more quickly, and stay there much longer than normal. This seems to be in part because you're able to **focus** again, keeping your rested and refreshed mind "on task" during your writing time. And most of all, the writing can become **FUN** again. And if it's fun, we want to write more, and more *often*, and the writing we produce tends to be our best.

Remember Samuel Butler's advice: "To do great work a man must be very idle as well as very industrious." Ask yourself: Are you doing great work? How industrious have you been lately? If the answers are negative, are you taking time to be idle? For more fun, focus, and "in flow" writing, want my advice? **Take some time off!**

A Writer's Courage

"**Y**ou need a certain amount of nerve to be a writer," author Margaret Atwood once said, "an almost physical nerve, the kind you need to walk across a river." Few writers would disagree, yet too many writers think it's their shameful little secret that they're scared.

Secret Fears

Fear is felt by writers at every level. Anxiety accompanies the first word put on paper—and the last, says Ralph Keyes in *The Courage to Write*. The courage demanded by writing, he says, is much like that of climbing a sheer granite cliff or skiing down a steep slope. This often surprises new writers. Beginning writers don't doubt that they have certain skills to learn. They expect to work hard in order to produce good writing. Their real shock, Keyes says, is discovering "how demanding writing is, not just of their skill, talent, and work ethic, *but of their valor.*"

Yes, valor. Nerve. Even heroism on some days! You're not alone with your fears. All writers are anxious, and there are many types of fears associated with writing. The good news is that those fears are both predictable and manageable.

Writer's Block?

Writers often mistakenly call fear writer's block, as if there's some clog in their literary pipe that can be cleaned out with a good dose of Drano. Many writers expect to cure this block by improving their writing techniques. We think that if we expand our vocabulary and smooth our transitions and use more detailed description, our confidence level will rise and the block will vanish.

> ***Too bad it doesn't work that way.***

Since this kind of writer's block doesn't arise from lack of skill, it's seldom eased by studying harder. Don't misunderstand me. Studying your craft will boost your confidence in your ability to get the words down as you write. It just won't conquer the fear that may have stopped you from writing in the first place—the fear of being honest.

Unvarnished Truth

Do we dare write from the heart, from the gut level of our emotions? Do we dare to call a spade a spade in our writing, saying what we really think instead of what we *should* think, and to heck with what our spouses or mothers-in-law might say? Do we suspect deep down that, if we could hide behind a pseudonym, our words might come out drastically different— stronger and more powerful, almost electric?

I know that I fear being totally honest. Do you? Try this experiment.

This Is Only a Test!

Choose a scene from a recent short story or chapter of your book in progress. See how graceful the prose, how politically correct the dialogue? See how the words flow in obedience to your hard-won craftsmanship? See the socially acceptable way in which the conflict is worked out? Now take that scene and pretend the story is going to be published under a phony name. It will be read very widely, but no one will know it's *you* behind the words.

If you write nonfiction, try the same thing with a passage from an article or book in which you've drawn an acceptable, conventional conclusion about some controversial facts.

This is the test: how much would you change if you were sure no one would know *you* had written it?

Now write your story or article that way.

This is where the courage comes in. It isn't usually our fear of using a wrong verb in a tag line, or mixing our metaphors, that produces the dreaded writer's block. We're afraid of being transparent, of letting others see inside us—and perhaps judge us.

Experiment now. Rewrite that scene or nonfiction passage. Let it rip from as deep down in your soul as you can reach. Remember, it's going to be published and read by thousands, but no one will ever know that you wrote it. With that in mind, what do you *truly* want to say?

Shocked?

If you take time to do this exercise, you may be astounded (as I was) at the difference in the writing. Is your second version stronger? Did you shock yourself anyplace? Did the original version coddle and soothe the reader, while this revision knocks his socks off? If so, you may have found your writing voice.

If you can find the inner courage to give expression to this true voice, chances are good that writer's block will be a thing of the past.

The Common Lot of Writers

Fears of all kinds surround writing. These fears are nearly universal, but so seldom discussed. New writers can hardly believe that seasoned writers—especially often published writers—could possibly have these fears. They do. They've just learned strategies to turn this anxiety-energy into words on a page. They're the ones who keep typing while their hearts race and go on submitting manuscripts even though their stomachs churn.

True Courage

Perhaps we need to redefine our terms. General Omar Bradley once said that courage is not the absence of fear, but the "capacity to perform properly even when scared half to death." That's the writing life in a nutshell.

The fact is that a state of anxiety (of varying degrees) is the writer's natural habitat. I hope this message comforts rather than discourages you. Trying to deny, avoid, or numb the fear of writing is neither possible nor desirable. Sounds inviting, doesn't it? Facing a lifetime of anxiety? Stewing in your writing juices hour after hour, day after day, year after year?

Transformation

Don't worry. It doesn't have to be that way. Your fears probably won't go away; what they will do is fuel your excitement for your writing project. Fear is pure energy, and it's an energy source that you can tap into and use (if you don't deaden it with sugar or alcohol or ignore it by taking a nap). It's a well-kept secret, but you **can** convert anxiety at each stage of your writing into one of your best sources of writing energy. Then you can get on with the courageous business of writing.

Epilogue

I hope *Writer's First Aid* has spurred you on to attempt your best writing. Sometimes I was your cheerleader, sometimes your mother, occasionally a mean cowpoke with a cattle prod. Most times, though, I was just a fellow writer because we're all in this together. We all have trouble getting started, we all struggle to create the writing life of our dreams, we all juggle our time and finances to make room for our writing "habit," and we all deal with a variety of fears and frustrations.

We keep on writing in spite of it all. Why? Why *should* we write? Writing is good for the soul and the spirit. Writing gives voice to our passions. Writing can ground us and help us untangle our lives. Being published gives us an audience, a way to share ourselves and help others. And making money at writing—getting paid for something you love to do—is one terrific way to earn a living.

Whatever your writing goals and dreams, I hope that *Writer's First Aid* helps you realize them and will be the book you reach for when you need comfort, aid, a gentle push, or an encouraging word. By definition, writers write. I hope my book helps you do just that.

Kristi Holl

Notes

Notes

Notes

Notes

Notes

Notes